The Essential Guide to Cybersecurity for SMBs

Gary Hayslip

Copyright © 2020 CISO DRG

The Essential Guide to Cybersecurity for SMBs

CISO DRG Publishing
8895 Towne Centre Drive, Suite 105 #199
San Diego, CA 92122
<www.CISODRG.com>
info@cisodrg.com
ISBN 978-0-9977441-6-3

DISCLAIMER: The contents of this book and any additional comments are for informational purposes only and are not intended to be a substitute for professional advice. Your reliance on any information provided by the publisher, its affiliates, content providers, members, employees or comment contributors is solely at your own risk. This publication is sold with the understanding that the publisher is not engaged in rendering professional services. If advice or other expert assistance is required, the services of a competent professional person should be sought.

To contact the authors, write the publisher at the address provided above, "Attention: Author Services."

Dedication

I want to dedicate this book to my best friend, my wife of 30 years, Sandi Hayslip. She has been with me through my time on active duty and its long deployments, always keeping our family strong. She is the rock that we gather around and the life friend I have the privilege to talk with on long walks. Her insight, strength, and faith have been examples for me to aspire towards, and I am grateful that she continues to encourage me to lead and stay engaged in our cyber community.

Acknowledgments

I want to acknowledge the following people for their contributions, directly or indirectly, in encouraging me, providing resource materials, assistance with proofreading the manuscript, and providing me coffee when I needed it:

Palmer Taskerud – you were there at the beginning, as my boss, mentor, and friend. It was your insight and the occasional smack in the back of the head that kept me honest. Thanks for pushing me out of the nest. It has been a fantastic ride, my friend.

Bill Bonney – for being a friend and brother in arms. Your level-headedness kept me focused and on task. I can't imagine the number of rabbit holes we've avoided.

Matt Stamper – for being a brother and close friend ready to stand in and swing a bat when needed. Your insight into privacy, risk, and compliance is always welcome, along with your snarky comments and corny jokes.

Macy Dennis – my brother, thank you for being the rock in hard times. I have truly appreciated your insight and suggestions that have helped me develop into a better security professional.

Julian Waits – brother, mentor, and friend who always has an insightful lesson to teach me, gained through hard-won experience. Thank you for helping me see the business side of cybersecurity and mature into the executive I have become.

How to Use this Book

This book is the first in a series of reference books for small business security professionals. It is written for the security professionals, managers, or CISO for Small and Medium Businesses (SMB)s that are between 50-500 employees. These are companies that are growing and as they have matured their business operations, they now must look to mature their approach to cybersecurity and managing their business risk.

I view the chapters contained in this book as separate discussions between you and I as we look at methods that you can use to build your first security program or improve a program already in place. It is my wish that through using this book you will improve as a security professional, and that your company and its operations will be more secure and your team and its members will mature and grow professionally.

Finally, even though this book can be viewed as a standalone guide for SMB security professionals it also should be considered as a companion guide to the CISO Desk Reference Guide Volumes 1 & 2. Please visit https://www.cisodrg.com for a complete catalog of our books.

Table of Contents

Introduction

As today's news reports of another data breach or company falling victim to cybercrime, small and medium-sized businesses now realize the ugly truth that they just as easily susceptible to cyber incidents. It was taken by many of them as a given that since they were small with few financial resources, they would be of no interest to cybercriminals. However, this viewpoint is changing as the recent Verizon data breach report of 2019[1] points out that SMB's are now targeted in increasing numbers. This report states that small businesses make up 58% of the reported data breaches for 2019, and the average cost per violation can equate to almost $3 million per incident. These costs include such expenses as forensic services, data restoration, customer notice, and credit monitoring, and are quite substantial to small businesses surviving on tight budgets.

I believe it is safe to say that it appears small- and medium-size companies are now considered by cybercriminals to be attractive targets of opportunity because of the perception that they have minimal security. Couple this perception with how many of these same small companies are doing business online using new technologies they may not fully understand, and this perception may also be a reality. Small businesses supply many larger organizations, resulting in possible connections to corporate networks that bring unforeseen risks.

It is with these risks in mind that I decided to write a book for security professionals tasked with protecting small businesses. I have collected many of the articles I have written over the last several years and put them in this book as a guide for the small business security professional. I believe a small business can reduce its risk and protect

---

[1] See reading list for Section 1

itself through implementing some basic security practices and accepting cybersecurity as a strategic business initiative. I hope that the essays included in this book provide both security professionals and executives of small businesses a blueprint of best practices to protect themselves and their customers.

Cybersecurity and the Business

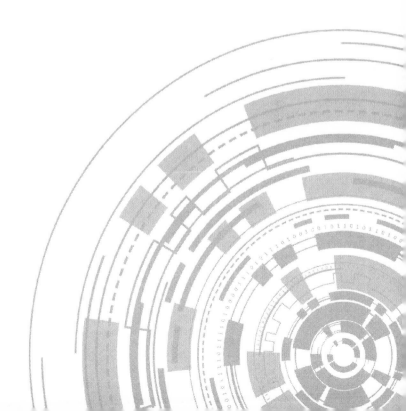

Introduction

The first section addresses the new reality facing SMBs. Everyone is a target and thieves will always attack what they perceive to be the easiest, fastest, or most lucrative opportunity.

Chapter 1 provides a four-section checklist that every SMB can use to make sure they have the basic program infrastructure in place. Chapter 2 lays out a tried and true approach to integrating your cyber program with the rest of the business. Critical to this outcome is learning to think about cyber in the business context, i.e., what is essential to the business and how your cyber program supports the business objectives.

In addition to understanding the value the business needs from the cyber program and making sure the infrastructure to support that is in place, the business must support the cyber program as well and Chapter 3 addresses how to build a cyber-aware culture.

At the end of Section 1 you will find a curated reading list to support you on your journey.

Chapter 1

The Essential Cybersecurity Checklist for SMBs

Ponemon Institute's State of Cybersecurity Report for small and medium-sized businesses (SMBs)[2] found that 67% of small businesses had experienced a cyber incident in the previous twelve months. Almost half of the respondents (47%) stated they lacked an understanding of how to protect their companies from a cyber incident. This finding is one of the reasons why I am writing this book, and this first chapter contains an essential checklist of practices and procedures that a security practitioner for SMBs along with their executive team can incorporate to enhance risk management controls for protecting business operations. This checklist is intended to be a basic template for evaluating what security controls and processes are currently in use and helping identify areas that need more attention.

1. Understand the Business and Business Continuity

This is not as hard as it sounds, but it will require some work to identify and track all critical business systems, processes, partners, and assets that may be susceptible to compromise. Think of this as putting together a list of the essential components that the business must have to operate in the event of an emergency. For the security leader at an SMB, it's critical to understand that you alone will not know what assets are essential, which is why it's crucial to work with the business to identify them and agree on the level of controls required for their safety. Some processes that I have found useful:

[2] *2018 State of SMB Sybersecurity*, Ponemon Institute, 2018
https://start.keeper.io/2018-ponemon-report

- Collect emergency contact information for critical employees and essential third-party personnel such as key customers, partners, services providers (including SaaS service providers), legal counsel, and law enforcement. You don't want to be in the middle of an incident struggling to find the needed contact information.

- Assist the business in developing the business operations plan:

  - ☐ Standard business procedures for normal operations.

  - ☐ Alternate business procedures for other-than-normal operations (for example, this may include procedures for incidents like loss of power, snow days, remote work, and loss of data centers).

  - ☐ Include a security addendum that documents current physical security measures and methods to replace these security controls if they are impacted in the event of an incident.

  - ☐ Business operations plans should acknowledge any compliance frameworks that apply to the organization, such as Sarbanes-Oxley (SOX), HIPAA, PCI DSS, CCPA, and GDPR.

- Develop a business continuity and disaster recovery plan:

  - ☐ Create emergency plans with critical suppliers and partners.

  - ☐ Create notification processes to alert customers.

  - ☐ Develop a dependency analysis that looks at critical parts of the business such as vendors, technology, services, staff, partners, etc. and have discussions about how the company would respond if they were lost.

  - ☐ Incorporate alternative business operations into this plan and then test them periodically; the norm is to do annual testing.

☐ Prepare for local emergency power generation, UPS, backup generators, etc., if necessary.

☐ Ensure that all critical IT equipment has Uninterruptible Power Supplies (UPS) with battery back-up and make sure to test them periodically.

☐ Develop procedures for offline financial transactions (e.g., cash, checks) if required and ensure that your financial institution is included in these procedures.

☐ Plan for moving business operations to an alternate facility, site, or cloud instance.

☐ Develop procedures for how business operations will be restored to normal.

☐ Plan for retrieving and restoring backup data.

- Train employees on business operations, business continuity, and disaster recovery plans

  ☐ Conduct training quarterly, bi-annually, annually, or as needed.

  ☐ Assess the overall training – conduct "lessons learned" debriefs.

  ☐ Use realistic practice drills, tabletops, and exercises, for training team members, employees, and trusted third parties.

2. Develop a Security Program

Hopefully, the business already has a security program in place, and this is just a review. If not, this tends to be more in-depth than the first practice of understanding the business. In this process, look at some of the underlying policies and programs that a security practitioner would need to begin implementing security practices into the business operations of their company and manage its risks.

- Develop and get approved at least these nine cybersecurity policies, including:

  ☐ Acceptable Use, Access Control, Change Management, Information Security, Incident Response, Remote Access, Email/Communication, Disaster Recovery, and Business Continuity. More to follow on these policies in subsequent chapters.

  ☐ Ensure employees are trained on each policy and have them sign an acknowledgment that they have read and understood them. This review should be conducted annually or as policies and business requirements change.

  An excellent reference for security policy templates is provided by SANS[3].

- Essential cybersecurity best practices to implement for reducing risk:

  ☐ Backup business data. Ensure the backups are encrypted, and copies are stored offsite. The significant issue here is if you encrypt, make sure you have control of your encryption keys, and periodically test your backups via a restoration process.

  ☐ Make sure all IT assets (desktops, laptops, servers, tablets, etc.) are protected (if applicable) with anti-virus and anti-malware security software that is configured for automated updates.

  ☐ Ensure all IT assets are updated with the current operating system and security patches on at least a monthly basis when operationally feasible.

  ☐ Secure wireless networks with strong passwords (remove factory defaults); hide the broadcast identifier (SSID) to

---

[3] *Information Security Policy Templates*, SANS 2019
https://www.sans.org/security-resources/policies

reduce "drive-by" attacks and incorporate the latest encryption protocols.

☐ Enable system and network audit logging where applicable and use a SIEM or log server to collect information for monitoring, detection, and remediation. Have this internally for your own team or have this capability for a third party that is providing security services.

☐ Review compliance framework security controls to ensure you are meeting relevant regulatory requirements (e.g., PCI, HIPAA, GDPR) and document this for audit purposes.

☐ Limit direct access to customer records and intellectual property to only those whose job role requires it for business reasons.

☐ If you use cloud-based "compute" services, implement a cloud access security broker (CASB) solution to monitor and manage internal traffic and data transfer to cloud-based sites and services.

☐ Implement an email security gateway to reduce malware and phishing emails received by employees. Select a solution that allows you to simulate phishing emails to train employees.

☐ Train employees at least annually in cybersecurity awareness and provide periodic training every month that covers cybersecurity topics to ingrain cybersecurity as part of the organization's business culture.

● Identify which of the above cybersecurity practices you are not able to provide and seek a managed service provider (MSP) or a managed security service provider (MSSP) to assist you in protecting your company, its employees, and critical business operations.

● Develop an incident management program:

☐ Maintain an updated configuration management database (CMDB) of computer assets (hardware and software).

☐ Maintain emergency contact information for all third-party partners, suppliers, and IT service providers.

☐ Create incident response runbook templates and train incident response teams regarding their responsibilities for such common incidents as lost IT asset or device, ransomware attack, distributed denial-of-service (DDOS), attack on e-commerce portal or company website, spear phishing attack, and malware attack.

☐ Establish notification procedures for executive staff, the business continuity team, third-party contractors, and employees.

☐ Define and establish priority notification of law enforcement, regulatory entities, and customers or clients, as deemed appropriate by management in consultation with legal counsel.

☐ Verify that incident response operations meet regulatory compliance requirements, such as GDPR's or CCPA's reporting timeline as an example (if required).

☐ Conduct incident response training with the business continuity and disaster response teams at least quarterly as a tabletop exercise and annually as a full exercise.

3. Actions to Follow During a Security Incident

With processes 1 and 2 in place, you should be in a better position to help the business manage its operations during a security incident. The following are some necessary actions for you to take; they should assist you in reducing the impact of a cybercriminal event on the company. Understand, this is by no means a complete list; it is just a reminder of incident response best practices that you, as the security team leader, will need to manage.

- Identify the compromised and impacted assets and assess the damage (verify whether protected data is involved, such as that defined by PCI, HIPAA, CCPA, or GDPR, as examples).

- Initiate the incident response plan to minimize business impact, and if this appears to be a business-wide event, contact the business continuity team manager to initiate emergency business contingency plans.

- Reduce damage by removing (disconnecting) affected computers, if applicable; this will depend on the type of incident, and if you are collecting live threat intelligence.

- Obtain and secure system configuration, network, and intrusion detection logs. Note any configuration changes (before and after the incident). Preserve hard drive(s) from the compromised system, if possible.

- Work with legal counsel to notify appropriate authorities, if necessary. If required, initiate a third-party retainer for forensic services and data retrieval operations.

4. Return to Normal Business Operations

Disaster recovery is typically managed by the IT department, however in SMBs it may include IT, cybersecurity, and third-party partners.

- Establish recovery points so that impacted systems are recovered in stages, and operations are gradually restored after testing.

- Take the necessary actions to restore systems to standard configurations. Use backup data to restore systems to last known "clean" status.

- Update restored systems with current data from manual transactions that may have occurred while systems were unavailable.

- Create a new "clean" backup after data has been updated.

- Re-establish normal business operations as soon as feasible; bring up critical systems and services first. Avoid running backup systems so long that you impact your ability to switch back to primary systems.

This template of actions to follow is not all-inclusive; it is an essential collection of steps organizations, and their security managers, can use to verify that they have the practices and written procedures in place to manage operations during a security incident. I highly recommended that SMBs establish a security program and start by designating an employee as the security manager. As the security manager, the employee will have overall responsibility for implementing cybersecurity best practices and working with peers to incorporate resiliency into critical business operations.

Chapter 2

Approaching Cybersecurity as a Critical Business Function

"I don't have to worry about cybercriminals; I am a small company. Why would they care about me?" I can't count the number of times I have heard a version of that statement. I have found that many SMBs don't see themselves as targets. I gather that in the digital hurricane that is today's internet, SMB leaders imagine themselves as debris that is so small, no one will notice. However, as we have seen in the Verizon data breach report[4], cybercrime is on the rise across all industries and company sizes, including SMBs. Couple this with the expansion of new malware types and the growth of cheap automated hacking tools; cybercriminals have it easier now than ever to search for new targets of opportunity.

With this growing threat in mind, I believe there are several reasons SMBs have increased exposure to cybercrime. One reason is that many have a minimal understanding of their company's risk exposure to current threats. Another reason is that many SMBs are constrained by resource availability, whether that is financial resources, trained security staff, or trusted partners. One final critical reason is that many feel spending scarce resources on security services could significantly impact their profitability. They face a decision to either pay for a security service to prevent something that may happen or use the needed funds to grow the business – typically growing the company wins. These negative drivers impair the ability of an SMB to respond to and survive a business-impacting

---

[4] *2019 Data Breach Investigations Report*, Verison 2019
https://enterprise.verizon.com/resources/reports/2019-data-breach-investigations-report.pdf

cybercrime incident, which is why I am writing this book as a primer for SMB security managers. This primer will contain basic security practices that can be used by a security manager to remediate risk exposure to critical data and business operations without having to incur high costs.

The following are four necessary security steps for SMB security managers to use in framing their discussion with company leadership on how to approach and implement cybersecurity as a core business function for all business initiatives.

1. Understand the Business Needs that Drive Cybersecurity Investments

Security managers need to understand why specific security controls and the associated security stack technologies are required and the value these services should provide. One of the first steps is for security managers to understand how their organization works as a business and what its core needs are before diving into using risk frameworks, implementing security controls, or applying best practices. Understanding how the business runs, along with critical information such as what data, operations, partners, and regulations are required to keep the company running, will help the security manager understand what is vital to the business. This will help them select appropriate cybersecurity requirements that enhance operations, not hinder them.

With this insight, the security manager for an SMB should now understand what controls and technologies meet their risk reduction needs without impeding current business initiatives. They can then start to implement security controls to protect their specific small business. I have found in the past this decision of where to start building a security stack with its control infrastructure is best done with input from stakeholders and peers from other internal departments who help the security manager understand their needs and what risks have priority.

When everything is done, the main focus here is for the security manager to protect the growing business and its critical assets through educating themselves on what is required by the company for it to operate effectively. Then with this insight, security managers help their company understand its current risk exposure, how much of that risk they are willing accept, and finally, what cybersecurity services the company is willing to implement based on its defined or agreed-to risk tolerances.

2. Review and Understand the Current IT Portfolio

After the SMB and its security manager understand their cybersecurity needs, there are initial steps that can be taken to identify and manage corporate risk exposure. The first step is to review the current information technology (IT) portfolio. This portfolio is an inventory of the existing IT environment, including hardware, software, network infrastructure, staff skill sets, third-party connections, third-party service providers, SaaS services, and remote workers or contractors. The reason for this first step is to ensure that the security manager understands the deployed technical landscape. This will allow the security manager to advise the leadership team about ongoing technical risks, the location and use of business data deemed critical for operations, and sensitive connections to partners or stakeholders outside the company. By the end of this step, the security manager will understand their IT environment's current state and have identified areas for improvement.

3. Conduct a Risk Assesment

The next step for an SMB's security manager is to talk with stakeholders and peers within the business and collaborate on a vision of the company's future state. Then with this vision, develop a plan with specific projects, initiatives, and metrics to attain that next level of maturity. To get there, the security manager will need to select a framework to conduct an organizational risk assessment. This assessment will provide a baseline of current security controls that are working correctly, controls that are immature needing remediation, and controls that don't apply to existing business operations. The results of this assessment will provide a more in-depth view of the risks facing the business. This new risk picture is then used to initiate further discussions into business practices that may need to be updated, new security technologies to be implemented, or security services that can be acquired from a trusted partner.

Getting this clear picture of risk helps establish the SMB's "risk appetite." It also provides the security manager with a methodology for how they will review future business opportunities using technology, processes, and security controls. Having this process in place allows an SMB's security manager to protect the company and manage its risks without impacting the organization's ability to be profitable.

4. Developing a Strategic Improvement Plan

As mentioned previously, in establishing a risk baseline, the security manager identifies business processes that need updating and security controls that are immature. These issues are a ready-made list for the business to develop a strategic plan for improving the company's security posture. This plan is created through a collaborative process where stakeholders and the security manager rank issues by priority based on their impact on business operations, value to business stakeholders, compliance or regulatory requirements, and finally, whether there is currently funding. The development of this strategic improvement plan enables the security manager and their team to understand what security initiatives to complete first, the value these projects bring to the company, and ongoing security controls that must be managed.

There's no denying that the number of breaches and attacks on the SMB community is continuing to grow. I believe in addressing these escalating risks. SMBs and their security managers can be proactive and manage their risk exposure through basic cybersecurity hygiene practices. Some recommended resources that can assist security practitioners in developing their first security strategy are listed in the Section 1 reading list.

Remember, cybersecurity is a lifecycle that doesn't provide value in a vacuum. For the SMB to be relatively safe, it must approach cybersecurity as a critical business function and trust its security manager.

Chapter 3

Building a Cyber-Aware Culture Is an Essential Business Initiative

Over the past decade, one of the core precepts that I have found to be either an asset or a barrier to me as a CISO was my company's internal business culture. Culture, by definition, is an organization's accepted norms, values, or behaviors. I heard it phrased as follows when I questioned a frustrated employee about not following the rules, "Well, why should I? It's not the way we do things around here." Whether you are a CISO for a large company or a security manager for an SMB, this pushback against best practice processes you are trying to implement is not a thing of the past. It is a continuing challenge.

The importance of this challenge for an SMB's security manager and security program can't be overstated. Couple this with the fact that security managers and their teams are considered change agents, and you have threats all around that must be managed. As you can imagine, changes like new policy guidelines, new regulations, or risk remediations don't go well when they collide with entrenched business culture. The security manager and team are resented for upsetting employees and changing their quiet norm. However, these changes, when properly evangelized to employees, can be useful for the business in time. The employees will be better for it too. What is needed is for the security manager to implement a process that first engages employees and builds trust.

It's this process of building trust and linking an SMBs culture to the value of cybersecurity that I want to discuss in this chapter. ISACA and CMMI conducted a "Culture of Cybersecurity" survey[5] where they asked several thousand cybersecurity professionals a series of questions about their organization's culture as it relates to being cyber-aware and whether this awareness was considered valuable. I found two of the survey's questions and their results to be startling. They highlight how organizations, large and small, need assistance in growing their internal business culture's acceptance of cybersecurity as part of the new business norm.

The first question was if companies believed an influential business culture that was cyber-aware of risks would increase the profitability or viability of the company. Across the spectrum of professionals surveyed, a healthy 87% felt that having a stronger cybersecurity culture would benefit the business. Now comes the exciting part. After this question, the surveyed security professionals were then asked a second question about what inhibits their businesses from achieving desired cyber awareness goals. The answers to this second question fell into two main camps. 41% of those surveyed stated that lack of employee buy-in or understanding was the main challenge for them. Another 39% stated that disparate business units, separated by styles, cultures, and regions, were why they were unable to incorporate cyber awareness into their business norms.

To sum this up, across the majority of those security professionals who participated in this survey, almost all of them stated they felt having more cyber awareness would be beneficial for their businesses. However, even though cyber awareness is considered good, they felt that employees' misunderstanding and entrenched cultural norms would prevent them from achieving their desired cybersecurity culture. I believe that the answers to the questions above demonstrate a disconnect that should inform how SMBs should approach becoming cyber-aware, and that illustrate the importance of business

---

[5] *Cybersecurity Culture Report,* ISACA 2018
   http://www.isaca.org/info/cybersecurity-culture-report/index.html

culture for security managers who are tasked to grow their security programs while still protecting the company.

Cyber awareness is an essential business asset, and when properly implemented and supported provides exceptional risk management value to the company. To begin taking advantage of this critical competency, the security manager needs to understand that changing culture requires two core items to be successful. The first is executive leadership support and the second is patience. Changing culture is not easy and takes time.

1. Baseline

To blend cyber awareness into a business's culture, and do so with minimal resistance, it's critical to establish a current baseline. In the past, as a CISO, I would start by discussing the merits of cyber awareness with my organization's executive leadership team and conducting a companywide awareness survey. This survey would document employees' current levels of knowledge about essential cybersecurity best practices, current threats, and applicable compliance requirements. The results of this survey would then be shared with the executive leadership team so they would understand the company's current level of cyber awareness and identify areas to be targeted for improvement.

2. Leadership Support Is Critical

Once the leadership team has been briefed, the security manager should discuss with them what an ideal cyber-aware culture looks like. Describe what resources are needed to begin any new initiatives, and what metrics and reports would be used to monitor the return on value to the business over time. To undertake cyber awareness initiatives, the security manager should request that their leadership team make a companywide announcement showing support for any new projects. Another effort to add to this companywide announcement would be the development of a charter from the business establishing the security program and outlining the support from the business's leadership team. For any efforts that require a culture change, the security manager needs to get employee buy-in, and one critical component that helps this acceptance by employees is the business's leadership team demonstrating its support not just once but continuously.

3. Not All Cyber Topics Are Created Equal

Now it's time to get started. The SMB's senior security professional will have conducted previous risk assessments that identified the company's essential assets (data, technology, and people) and any compliance requirements it must meet. The survey results and its information will help the security manager evaluate what types of training their SMB's employees will require, and any specialized training (cases in point could include PCI and HIPAA) needed for specific business units. I would also recommend that the security team reach across the company and select a range of people to help determine the training topics and best delivery methods for employees. What is crucial here is that these initiatives need to be relevant, they need to resonate with employees and make sense, and the methods to deliver this training should engage employees. Getting employees involved in building the cyber-aware process helps with buy-in and allows the security manager and team to build trust.

4. Launching a Cyber-Aware Culture

The initial cyber-aware topics and interactive content deployment methodology have been selected. It's now time to test it on a select group of employees to verify that after the training they understand how their previous inactions exposed the organization to risk, and how their new knowledge helps protect them, the company, and their families. This stage of building a cyber-aware culture may require the test group to evaluate different training platforms until one is identified that makes the training impactful and relevant. Experience has shown that employees hate watching videos and answering questions. However, they do like interactive training that requires some hands-on experience and resonates with real-time events or scenarios that they remember, and information that can be used not just in their job but in their own lives outside of work.

5. It's About Building Trust

The training topics and learning management platform have been tested and approved. It's now time for your SMB to deploy the security training to all employees. This includes the executive leadership team on down to the newest employee. Remember, as a security leader, you are trying to change the culture. This effort will require more than just an annual training class; it will require surveys, lunch-n-learns, blogs, posters, mini-training sessions, and for the security team to get out of their work areas and be visible. Employees must feel comfortable making mistakes and reporting issues. Security team members must accept the fact that employees are their customers, and they are there to serve them. Executive leadership must provide consistent advocacy of cyber awareness initiatives and lead by example. They must demonstrate that they follow established best practices and be willing to state they are suitable for the company. Finally, the security manager must use metrics and data collected during training to show how the acceptance of cyber awareness as part of the business has reduced risk through fewer incidents, data compliance issues, and risky behaviors.

Remember, a culture of cyber awareness is attainable. It takes everyone in the company to be part of the process, and it takes continuous advocacy of its benefits for it to be accepted as the new norm. You must incorporate cyber awareness as part of your overall security program and be willing to take the time required to build trust.

Reading List for Section 1

1. *2018 State of SMB Sybersecurity*, Ponemon Institute, 2018
   https://start.keeper.io/2018-ponemon-report

2. *Information Security Policy Templates*, (SysAdmin, Audit, Network, Security (SANS) Security Resources, 2019
   https://www.sans.org/security-resources/policies

3. *2019 Data Breach Incidents Report*, Verizon, 2019
   https://enterprise.verizon.com/resources/reports/2019-data-breach-investigations-report.pdf

4. *Implementing Cybersecurity Guidance for Small and Medium-Sized Enterprises,* Information Systems Audit and Control Association (ISACA), 2015.

5. *CyberSecure My Business.*, Stay Safe Online, 2019
   https://staysafeonline.org/cybersecure-business/

6. *Cybersecurity Culture Report,* ISACA 2018
   http://www.isaca.org/info/cybersecurity-culture-report/index.html

Foundational Elements

Section 2 lays out the foundational elements of your program. Start with a gap analysis, using Chapter 4 as your guide. This does not have to take months of time and hundreds of person hours, but neither is it a back-of-the-envelope exercise. With good planning and executive support, you can conduct a timely and inclusive assessment.

Chapter 5 reveals the basics of cyber hygiene. Taken individually, cyber controls can often seem unnecessary and burdensome, but taken together as a whole, an investment in strong cyber hygiene provides a solid foundation for your program.

Chapter 6 then shows you how to codify the policies and procedures in support of your cyber hygiene program. In addition to documenting how your program is administered and prescribing the controls to be executed, policies and procedures create the program elements that auditors and regulators require to examine and signoff on your program.

Multiple policy examples are referenced in chapter 6. The citations are provided as footnotes and links valid as of this publication date are provided in the curated reading list at the end of Section 2.

Chapter 4

Conducting a Security Gap Analysis

As a security leader, one of the most critical aspects of managing an SMB's security program is understanding its risk exposure and any inconsistencies (gaps) in security control coverage. As I have stated in previous chapters, these inconsistencies are troubling for a security leader and can have detrimental effects on a growing SMB. Understanding their context and impact on business operations is crucial for the maturity of the security program and the organization's overall health.

To address gaps in your security program, you will have typically conducted a risk assessment and then have processed the results. Many in the cybersecurity community know this process of evaluation and review as performing a "gap analysis." For this process to be considered unbiased, it is typically conducted by an independent or impartial resource such as an external partner or an internal resource not directly involved in security operations. No matter the approach that the business selects for conducting a gap analysis, the result should be a report that highlights findings to include risks, recommendations, and any compliance requirements.

For security managers, the gap analysis is a strategic tool that provides dividends for security programs in many ways. As both a CIO and CISO, I have used this tool in the past to establish a risk baseline for my security and risk management programs. I have used it to document improvements in current security initiatives and to highlight how security provides value to the company or organization by reducing hazards to critical business processes. It is essential for you as your company's senior security leader to understand the gap analysis process so you can educate your leadership team about its value, and so they can champion your remediation efforts. These efforts and the resulting data analysis will provide the SMB's leadership team with visibility into the business risks, enabling them with your insight to make better, more informed decisions on how these risks should be managed.

The process of conducting a gap analysis covers numerous stages and will be different for each organization due to company maturity, business operations, and compliance requirements. With this in mind, I want to provide you with some necessary steps that security managers for an SMB should expect an assessor (internal or third-party) to follow in conducting a gap analysis of current security and risk management controls.

1. Obtain management support

If you want to be effective and make improvements, then you will need support from executive leadership. I would propose that you do this type of assessment annually at a minimum and use the results as part of the security program's report to the board or management team on the current risk exposures to operations.

2. Define the scope and objective

What is essential to note here is that the gap analysis process can cover the entire security program and its controls, or it can select a specific segment to assess. In doing a partial assessment, businesses can save time and resources, and if it doesn't go well, then a decision can be made on whether to conduct a full assessment and gap analysis. The security manager, assessor, and stakeholders will select the risk framework and methodology to use for the evaluation and identify the resources that will be required. *Note: For an SMB, the framework selected is usually based on the business's regulatory or compliance requirements.*

3. Create an assessment schedule

Now that the assessor has the plan components, it's time to put them together so that the security manager and the SMB have a schedule of events for the assessment and a projected timeframe to review results. I have seen assessments fall apart despite having the best methodology, tools, and people because the assessor never put together a plan that accounted for current business operations. When the assessors came on-site to start, they found that what they wanted to do for the assessment impacted the business units, and the whole process quickly ground to a halt. Remember, the purpose of the gap analysis is to identify risk hazards, not create them, so whether you are using someone internally to assess or a third party consider the impact on daily operations.

4. Review and agree on the assessment plan

As with the previous step, after the assessment team has created its plan, it needs to be given to the security manager and business stakeholders. This action will ensure that all parties who are part of the review understand the schedule and the processes to communicate any problems. It is critical for the success of this initiative that everyone understands the assessment plan and agrees to help with the process. Ensuring everyone understands the process is very import for you as a security manager because if the assessor wants to review and speak with people in other departments, it will be your responsibility to make sure it happens promptly without interfering with operations. Expect to be busy; you may not be doing the assessment, but you will be actively involved in the process.

5. Conduct information gathering

Information gathering will be one of the most tedious parts of the whole assessment. Typically, depending on the framework the security manager and organization selected, the assessor will use a security control matrix as a template to grade how well the business is implementing its security controls. The information collected about the specific area under review will consist of reports and documentation on whether a security control or process is in place and its level of maturity.

6. Interview key stakeholders

Part of collecting information for the assessment involves interviewing critical stakeholders across business units and other teams. Sometimes a security control is not a piece of technology but a business process. To assess how well that process is being followed, the assessor needs to speak with employees. Note that this shouldn't be an adversarial discussion but rather a quick review to validate that the employee understands the policy/process and can demonstrate they are following it correctly. As the security manager for the SMB, it will be part of your responsibility to make sure the stakeholders are available for these interviews.

7. Review supporting documentation

This part of the gap analysis process is where assessors work with the security manager and security team to answer questions about the collected findings. It is at this stage that the assessors may want to talk about some of the issues they have noted and ask about any documentation or information that can be used to clarify the discovered hazards. The assessor must spend time in this stage collecting as much information as possible to provide an accurate risk picture for the SMB.

8. Verify the information collected

All of the hard work is almost completed with the risk assessment. However, the assessor now has a large amount of data that must be reviewed to verify its applicability to the gap analysis process. When I have done risk assessments for companies in the past, I sometimes inadvertently collected information on procedures or business units that were not in scope for an assessment. It's in this stage that the assessor should remove these types of inconsistencies. An important outcome of this stage is that the data being reported is accurate and applies to the agreed-upon scope and objectives.

9. Note potential risks

The next step is to note the gaps in the standing security controls and associated security practices. The assessor takes the business' selected risk management framework and notes the security controls that were missing, immature, or misconfigured. When I have done risk assessments for companies in the past, I liked to list the issues with a security control and explain the impact to business operations if a cyber criminal exploited the control. This explanation helps provide the business context to the security manager and stakeholders and will help them prioritize which issues should be remediated first.

10. Document your findings

By this stage, the assessment is completed, and all of the results need to be collected and documented. The size of the risk assessment effort will dictate how long it will take to review all of the information and have it reviewed by a second source to confirm its validity. Usually, the assessor will go back to their company or department and begin to write up their findings. What is important here is that the security manager remains available to answer any questions to ensure the conclusions are as accurate as possible.

11. Develop the assessment report with recommendations

As we wrap this process up, the assessor develops a report for the security manager and the SMB's leadership team. Usually, the report will have multiple parts. The first section of the report is prepared for high-level executives and is short and to the point. It will state the objectives of the assessment, the methodologies that were used, and the final standings (gap analysis) concerning the company's overall risk baseline. The second part of the report is where the assessor goes in-depth, explaining each of the processes used to measure risk, findings for each segment under review, and references used to validate security controls and their maturity. The final section of the report offers recommendations to remediate findings. Again, this section will list multiple references and can be very technical in the analysis of risk hazards. Note that each part is for a different audience. In writing these types of reports, I have found I am most effective when I take my information and look at it through the lens of telling a business value story about risk. It's best to keep it simple and not get lost in the minutia of data.

12. Present report and get acceptance

The final step in conducting a gap analysis is for the assessor to present their findings. It is a best practice that the organization reviews the report and asks questions to understand the findings before accepting the conclusions. It is also a good idea for the security manager to be at this meeting to address the findings and answer their leadership team's questions. It is also quite common for the security manager or CISO to submit a preliminary report detailing how the findings will be remediated with a timeline so that a request for resources can be made if required. Each organization is different, but as a security manager, you should be prepared and have a remediation plan ready.

At first blush this whole practice may seem convoluted, but it is actually quite easy to follow once you have done it a couple of times. If this is new for you as a security manager, I would suggest using a trusted third party the first time, so you become familiar with the process. Many businesses know they need to do risk assessments to meet regulatory requirements but fail to do so because they don't grasp the value of the assessment process or know where to begin.

Businesses also often take issue with the findings of their gap analysis reports, uncertain about how to take the information and make it actionable to manage their company's risk. This reluctance is why I wanted to provide this basic methodology for the security manager to follow so it can be used to educate the SMB on the value of conducting their first risk and gap analysis.

Chapter 5

Understanding Cyber Hygiene: It's About the Basics

In the early morning hours, a security manager from a local SMB wakes up with her cell phone chirping. As she quickly looks at the offending device, she realizes it's a text message from one of her organization's vendors who provides cybersecurity services. As she rolls over and makes the phone call, she realizes she has an issue that will require her to wake up her team and start the day earlier than planned. As she speaks to her team over a hastily arranged video conference, it's soon apparent that there is a critical security patch that must be implemented as quickly as possible. Her security team members are concerned because this patch is to fix a recently discovered zero-day attack and they are worried that if it is not addressed soon, there may be unforeseen repercussions.

As her day unfolds and this issue is scheduled for change management and then later remediated by her team, she thinks about what it would be like to manage a network without standard security controls and policies. A network where standard security frameworks and industry best practices for managing risk are not followed and a simple phishing email, received by an employee, could have devastating consequences. This scenario is quite common – cybersecurity doesn't sleep, and neither do security professionals <smile>. What is vital for you to understand from this brief view into a security professional's life is that without standards, without basic security controls, without security hygiene, this story could have been much worse, and the security manager's company may have been severely impacted.

In today's interconnected world, phishing emails and malware infections caused by attachments and links to hacked web sites are just some of the digital debris that has become an everyday occurrence. However, in the disparate enterprise environments found in many small businesses, cities, and corporate networks, these types of attacks can be catastrophic due to the natural blending of old and new technologies. The repercussions of modern malware attacks on these intertwined infrastructures can result in loss of critical services to businesses and their customers.

To counter these ever-evolving threats, I believe organizations, and especially SMBs, who have limited resources should focus on doing the essential security controls well. Businesses must lay the equivalent of a digital foundation on which they can then build their networks and securely provide data and applications to their employees and customers. The methodologies that businesses and their security managers would follow to do the basics are commonly referred to as "cyber hygiene." There are numerous approaches to implementing cyber hygiene, and there are quite a few ideas for what should be considered cyber hygiene. What is essential for you to understand is that cyber hygiene isn't hard and can be managed through six necessary steps. The steps an SMB's security manager can use to protect the business are as follows: *Count, Configure, Control, Patch, Protect, and Repeat.*

The first step in implementing cyber hygiene, *"Count"* many would think should be pretty straightforward; however, having an accurate inventory can be extremely difficult. It is tough to protect an organization and establish an accurate risk baseline if there is poor visibility into what is connected to the business' networks. I previously recommended that you conduct an inventory by collecting information about current policies and procedures for how cybersecurity is managed in the organization. I then stated you and the business must review and update previous asset inventories for both hardware and software, and any current network documentation. With this updated information, not only are you prepared to meet critical cyber hygiene requirements, but you can also map and monitor the networks for a better view of its data flows and current architecture. What is crucial for you as the security manager for an SMB is to put together an accurate map of the organization's enterprise networks and a definitive list of its applications, hardware, and data types that are required by your business units. This collected information will become the technology and application portfolios of the organization. This data is essential for conducting business impact analyses and will be critical for implementing the steps to follow.

The next step for an SMB's security team to follow in implementing cyber hygiene, "*Configure*" is about understanding which settings all connected network devices have enabled and which settings are recommended for optimal performance. I recommend reviewing the CIS Benchmarks™ [6] website for best-practice configuration settings. To do configuration properly using recommended industry security settings as a baseline is considered standard. Once completed, it is incumbent on the security team to adjust ("tune") the controls to a "more secure" environment based on the criticality of your business operations and its data. Typically, organizations will have a standard operating system image preconfigured with all required security settings and required applications.

What is vital in this step is flexibility. As a security professional for a small business, you should make sure you don't miss even minor issues like changing preconfigured default security passwords. These can easily be found on the Internet and could be used against your company. Take the time for small things. As you change the default passwords, don't forget to review and change default security settings as well. These changes are all part of the "tuning" process to adjust configuration settings to your business, and once done, don't forget that all configurations and operating system images should now be backed up and continuously maintained. I would recommend storing them in a configuration management database (CMDB). By the end of this step, you will, as the security leader for your business,

---

[6] https://www.cisecurity.org/cis-benchmarks/

have ensured a level of maturity that will help your company as it implements new technologies to be competitive and increase its market share. As you finish this step, I would recommend you apply a policy to continually scan your business environment for assets that are misconfigured or missing software updates. These types of vulnerabilities expose your organization to risk, and ensuring you have updated assets with the correct configurations will reduce this exposure and any potential impact on business operations. Congratulations, you have two steps implemented. Let's now move to a more challenging one – control.

This third step "*Control*" is about building a cyber hygiene program that has a process for managing who has access to the settings implemented in "*Configure.*" It is also about gaining insight into the employees and vendors within the business that have administrator privileges to the company's assets and networks. These "admin" privileges can make enterprise changes, access critical data, and implement system-wide policies that would affect the business's ability to operate effectively. In this step, it's recommended that the SMB's security leader start with an audit to see who has administrative privileges or any elevated access.

Once that audit has been completed and the results compiled into a list, the security leader should then speak with the users to understand their business reasons for requiring these privileges. Once the audit findings have been remediated down to only essential personnel, I would then recommend that you as the security leader for your business implement a policy stating administrator accounts are to only be used for specific business purposes and administrators are to conduct all routine work-related activities with their separate standard user accounts. This policy can be an independent access policy, or it can be part of your Information Security Policy. What is important is that you standardize the use of these accounts so all personnel who have them understand and accept responsibility for using them. Now with this updated list of admin accounts documented and a policy in place for their use, you will need to periodically audit them to continually manage who has administrative rights and remove them when they are no longer needed. Don't be surprised that over time, the number of personnel with these elevated accounts grows, which is why you must periodically audit them to reduce this risk exposure to your business. Note that the security team should use technologies to automate the process of managing these administrator accounts. This process provides the security team with the ability to audit who is using these elevated rights and for what purpose, so if this account management is an issue for your company you may want to invest in this type of security control as your company matures.

The fourth step in the cyber hygiene process, "*Patch*" is critical for all organizations that use technology, and it is one of the hardest issues security leaders face – helping the business and IT teams standardize the process for how software updates will be regularly tested and applied to deployed applications, operating systems, and hardware. There are many documented data breaches that when triaged were traced back to a software patch not being correctly installed or not installed at all. What is essential for an SMB's leadership team and security manager to understand is that in cyber hygiene this step impacts all others. They must have a standardized process in place, so patches are installed correctly and timely. I would recommend at least a monthly patch management cycle, and adjust it depending on business requirements. There are numerous articles and books on how to create a patch management program, so I won't delve into this process here; remember, you need this control in place for all other cyber hygiene steps to function effectively.

The next step in implementing your cyber hygiene program, "*Protect*" is about using basic security applications and controls to set the first layer of protection so that a mature cybersecurity program can be built. It is in "Protect" that the SMB's security team will ensure endpoint protection is installed and updated on all desktops, laptops, servers, and mobile devices, if possible. As the security manager, you should also ensure that desktop firewalls or their equivalent are turned on and configured, hard drives have full disk encryption installed, and there is a password management program in place. This password management program should ensure there is some level of complexity to passwords and, if possible, use two-factor authentication for an additional level of authentication. Some additional services you would find managed in this step are verifying that all devices are generating some log data to be collected by a Security Information and Event Management (SIEM) solution and analyzed for abnormalities, the use of multi-factor authentication (MFA) for admin/privileged accounts, and finally, all critical data is backed up and the backups and their restoration are periodically tested. Now I understand that as a security manager working for an SMB, you may not be able to perform all of these "Protect" controls. If that is the case, I would recommend you identify what you can do and then look to a trusted partner like an MSSP to manage the rest.

The final step in our discussion on cyber hygiene, "*Repeat*" is about the need for you as the security manager to monitor and assess the selected and implemented security controls continuously. Networks are dynamic; they regularly change over time as updates are installed, configurations are changed or enabled, or new technologies are implemented. Just because your company is a small business doesn't mean its networks are any different; they will experience changes and flex as the business grows, so be ready for it and manage the risks. I would recommend in managing these risks that you don't keep them inside your security program but instead share them with your employees. I have found that training your employees to understand risks and establishing a continuous improvement process enables organizations to manage the risk of their installed technology portfolios and determine what risk is acceptable for business operations.

The above methods give small businesses and their security teams visibility into how their enterprise environments are built, how data is used by their stakeholders, and which older technologies may need to be updated or replaced. In the end, these six steps are just that, tools that security managers can use to create an underlying methodology for protecting their company and its operations. Once these basic processes and controls are in place, I recommend that as the security leader for your company you take the management of risk to the next level and use a mature cybersecurity/risk management framework to provide your security program with a strategic roadmap that can be followed to protect your company.

In the reading list for Section 2 you will find seven excellent site references to help organizations establish a security program.

Chapter 6

Policies and Procedures Recommended for a New Security Program

As the security manager for your small business, there comes a time when the company has grown to the point that common procedures need to be documented. This is a requirement of mature security programs – to develop and publish information security policies and plans. Policies are high-level documents created to provide an enterprise-level view of how your security program will provide a particular service. A plan is a step-by-step guide to how your team will execute a particular process. The value of these policies and plans is they provide visibility to the business and employees on how the security team manages the SMB's risks to operations and assets. Building and managing a security program is an effort that most organizations grow into over time, and they will rely on security professionals like yourself to not only create these policies and plans but keep them current.

As a security executive, I have worked with startups who had no rules for how assets or networks were used by employees, and I have worked at established organizations where every aspect of IT and cybersecurity was heavily managed. I found that the goal for CISOs and security managers such as yourself is to seek a middle ground where companies can responsibly manage their risk. In establishing the foundation for a security program, companies will usually start by designating an employee to be responsible for cybersecurity. It will be this employee who will begin the process of creating a policy and its associated plan to manage their company's risk through selecting security technologies, implementing security controls, auditing repeatable work processes, and documenting procedures. This chapter is about the core set of policies/plans that an SMB's security manager should have for a maturing security program.

1. Acceptable Use Policy (AUP)

An AUP stipulates the constraints and practices that an employee using organizational IT assets must agree to as a requirement for accessing the corporate network or the internet. These policies are common throughout industry and are typically provided as part of the onboarding process for new employees. New employees are usually given an AUP to read and sign before being granted a network ID. I recommend that the organization's IT, security, legal, and HR departments discuss what should be included in this policy in order to keep up with the ever-changing requirements that businesses must adhere to. An example of an AUP that is available for fair use can be found at SANS[7].

2. Access Control Policy (ACP)

The ACP outlines the account access procedures available to all employees who must connect to an organization's data and information systems. Some topics that are typically included in the policy are access control standards such as those documented in NIST's Access Control and Implementation Guides[8] (Dr. Vincent Hu, 2018). Other items covered in this policy are standards for user access, network access controls, operating system software controls, and the complexity requirements for corporate passwords. Additional items often outlined in ACPs include methods for monitoring how corporate systems are accessed remotely, how unattended workstations should be secured (e.g., system time out settings), and how and when access is removed when employees leave the organization. An excellent example of this policy is available at

---

[7] *Information Security Policy Templates,* SANS 2019, Security Policy Research
[8] *Access Control Policy and Implementation Guides,* Hu, Dr. Vincent 2018

the International Association of Privacy Professionals (IAPP) website[9].

3. Change Management Policy

A change management policy refers to a formal process for making changes to IT, software development, and security services and operations. The goal of a change management program is to increase the awareness and understanding of proposed changes across an organization and to ensure that all changes are conducted methodically to minimize any adverse impact on services and customers. The goal of change management is to control risk. A good description of change management for IT and Information Security can be found in the IT Infrastructure Library (ITIL)[10]. An excellent example of an IT change management policy available for fair use can be found at SANS[11].

4. Information Security Policy

Writing an information security policy for an SMB can be very simple. Remember, the document is typically kept at a high level and briefly covers the security controls that you have implemented to protect the business. This primary information security policy is developed by you as the security manager and socialized by leadership to ensure that across the organization, all employees who use corporate IT assets or its networks comply with its stated rules and guidelines. It is a good practice for you to ask your company to have employees read and sign this document, acknowledging they have read it (which is generally done in conjunction with reading and signing the AUP policy). This policy is designed to inform employees

---

[9] *Information Systems Access Policy*, IAPP 2016

[10] *What is IT Service Management*, AXELOS 2019

[11] *Sample IT Change Management Policies and Procedures Guide*, SANS 2007

that even at an SMB, there are rules that they will be held accountable for concerning the sensitivity of the corporate information and IT assets. The London School of Economics and Political Science provides an excellent example of a cybersecurity policy that is available for review[12].

5. Incident Response (IR) Policy

The incident response policy is an organized approach to how the company will manage an incident and remediate the impact on operations. It is a high-level document and typically enumerates all of the teams that will assist with the incident response process. A more in-depth document that explains the play-by-play of how the business will respond to incidents is the incident response plan; that document is also the responsibility of the security manager. The incident response policy is one policy CISOs and security managers hope never to use. However, the goal of this policy is to describe the process of handling an incident with the objective of limiting the damage to business operations and customers while reducing recovery time and costs. Carnegie Mellon University provides an example of a high-level IR plan[13] and SANS offers a plan specific to data breaches[14].

6. Remote Access Policy

The remote access policy outlines and defines acceptable methods of remotely connecting to an organization's internal networks. I have also seen this policy include addendums with rules for the use of BYOD (bring your own device) assets. This policy is a requirement for organizations that have dispersed networks with the ability to extend into insecure network locations, such as the local coffee house or unmanaged home networks. I have also seen this policy used to

---

[12] *Information Security Policy*, London School of Economics and Political Science, 2019

[13] *Computer Security Incident Response Plan*. Carnegie Mellon University, 2015

[14] *Data Breach Response*, SANS 2019

document how contract employees will access corporate networks. Some policies include which tools are acceptable for access. An example of a remote access policy is available at SANS[15].

7. Email and Communication Policy

A company's email policy formally outlines how employees can use the business' chosen electronic communication medium. As a security manager for an SMB, this document may not be required until the company grows, but it is an excellent policy to have in place to make sure business information is not transferred to personal email or social media accounts. I have also seen this policy cover more than just email accounts. It should also cover communication and collaboration technologies such as blogs, RSS feeds, social media platforms, and chat technologies. The primary goal of this policy is to provide guidelines to employees on what is considered acceptable and unacceptable uses of corporate communication technology. An example of an email and communication policy is available at SANS[16].

8. Disaster Recovery Policy

An organization's disaster recovery policy will generally include both the cybersecurity and IT teams' input for returning to normal business operations and will be developed as part of the broader business continuity policy. As the security manager for an SMB you and your team will manage an incident through your incident response plan, which will be your roadmap to follow in an incident. This disaster recovery policy provides a broader view of all stakeholders involved during an incident and helps you as a security leader understand where your team fits into the operational scheme of the business responding to an incident. Typically, if the event has

---

[15] *Remote Access Policy*, SANS 2019
[16] *Email Policy*, SANS 2019

a significant business impact you will report it to your leadership team, and the business continuity policy and its operational plan will be activated. Once the cyber incident is considered resolved, the disaster recovery policy and its operational plan will be activated to return business operations to normal. An example of a disaster recovery policy is available at SANS[17].

9. Business Continuity Plan (BCP)

The BCP will coordinate efforts across the organization and will use the disaster recovery plan to restore hardware, applications, and data deemed essential for business continuity. BCPs are unique to each business because they describe how the organization will operate in an emergency. An excellent example of a BCP template that organizations can use to create their own BCP is available at FEMA[18].

These policies and documents are just some of the basic guidelines I would recommend that security professionals at SMBs develop to build an effective security program. There are more that you will need to develop as your company matures, and hopefully, your security program will mature with it.

There are two resources I would recommend to security professionals who have been selected to create their company's first security policies. The first, as highlighted above, is the SANS Information security policy templates website with numerous plans available for download. Another source I would recommend is an article in CSO Magazine titled *Security*[19] that lists links for policies focused on unique issues such as privacy, workplace violence, and cellphone use while driving, to name a few.

In closing this discussion, remember that as the senior security leader for your company, it will be incumbent on you to evangelize your new policies and guidelines with employees. Employees must be

---

[17] *Disaster Recovery Plan Policy*, SANS 2019
[18] *Business Continuity Plan*, FEMA 2019
[19] *Security*, CSO Magazine, January 25 2016

aware of all current IT and cybersecurity procedures, and they must be trained and provided information so that security is seen as an "everyone" process.

Reading List for Section 2

1. *CIS Benchmarks*™, Center for Internet Security
   https://www.cisecurity.org/cis-benchmarks/

2. *Home and Business Security Resources*, Cybersecurity and Infrastructure Security Agency, 2019
   https://www.us-cert.gov/home-and-business
   Explore the resources in this section to learn more about cybersecurity and to better secure your home and small-business networks.

3. *An Introduction to Information Security*, National Institute of Standards and Technology (NIST), 2017
   https://csrc.nist.gov/publications/detail/sp/800-12/rev-1/final
   NIST SP 800-12 provides an excellent introduction to information security principles.

4. *Resources for Business*, Cybersecurity and Infrastructure Security Agency (CISA), 2019
   https://www.us-cert.gov/ccubedvp/getting-started-business
   Resources available to businesses and aligned to the five NIST Cybersecurity Framework Function Areas.

5. *Tips*, Cybersecurity and Infrastructure Security Agency, 2019
   https://www.us-cert.gov/ncas/tips
   Tips describe and offer advice about common security issues for non-technical computer users.

6. *Avoiding Social Engineering and Phishing Attacks*, Cybersecurity and Infrastructure Security Agency, 2019
   https://www.us-cert.gov/ncas/tips/ST04-014
   Good information defining social engineering and phishing emails.

7. *Securities Industry and Financial Markets Association: Resources*, SIFMA 2019
   https://www.sifma.org/cybersecurity-resources/

SIFMA has developed this Small Firms Cybersecurity Guidance to provide information to small firms to increase their security.

8. *Information Security Policy Templates*, SANS 2019
   https://www.sans.org/security-resources/policies

9. *Information Systems Access Policy*, IAPP 2016
   https://iapp.org/media/pdf/resource_center/AWPHD-ISaccess.pdf

10. *What is IT Service Management*, AXELOS 2019
    https://www.axelos.com/best-practice-solutions/itil/what-is-it-service-management

11. *Sample IT Change Management Policies and Procedures Guide*, SANS 2007, Cybersecurity Summit Archive
    https://www.sans.org/cyber-security-summit/archives/file/summit-archive-1493830822.pdf

12. *Information Security Policy*, London School of Economics and Political Science, 2019
    https://info.lse.ac.uk/staff/services/Policies-and-procedures/Assets/Documents/infSecPol.pdf

13. *Computer Security Incident Response Plan*, Carnegie Mellon University, 2015
    https://www.cmu.edu/iso/governance/procedures/docs/incident responseplan1.0.pdf

14. *Data Breach Response*, SANS 2019
    https://www.sans.org/security-resources/policies/general/pdf/data-breach-response

15. *Remote Access Policy*, SANS 2019
    https://www.sans.org/security-resources/policies/network-security/pdf/remote-access-policy

16. *Email Policy*, SANS 2019
    https://www.sans.org/security-
    resources/policies/general/pdf/email-policy

17. *Disaster Recovery Plan Policy*. SANS 2019
    https://www.sans.org/security-
    resources/policies/general/pdf/disaster-recovery-plan-policy

18. *Business Continuity Plan*, FEMA 2019
    https://www.fema.gov/media-library-data/1389019980859-
    b64364cba1442b96dc4f4ad675f552e4/Business_ContinuityPla
    n_2014.pdf

19. *Security,* January 25, 2016
    https://www.csoonline.com/article/3019126/security-policy-
    samples-templates-and-tools.html

The Cybersecurity Program

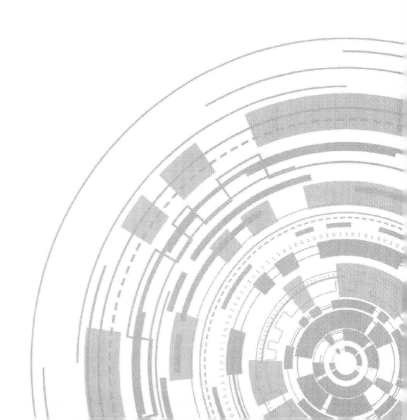

Introduction

Now that you have established how your program supports the organization and how the organization supports your program, and laid the groundwork for your program, it's time to put the specific processes in place.

Chapters 7 & 8 address one of your most important assets...data. In addition to the value your company places on data, state regulators are demanding a more systematic approach to data governance and now require that you transfer rights to the subject of the data.

Chapter 9 provides five key actions to create your program, while chapters 10 and 11 address threat intelligence and incident management, the programs for which most of your business partners will judge the effectiveness of your function.

A curated reading list again follows this section.

Chapter 7

Data Privacy, a Growing Strategic Initiative

January 28 is Data Privacy Day. It is observed internationally to raise awareness about the importance of respecting privacy, safeguarding data, and facilitating trust. In our current dynamic business environment, whether you are an SMB or a multinational corporation, everything is connected, and millions of businesses are unaware of or uninformed about how their personal and business information is being used, collected, or shared. The aggregation of new threats, laws, and consumer activism makes data privacy a strategic initiative for today's SMBs to understand and incorporate as part of their core business operations.

In a recent study conducted by the Ponemon Institute on SMBs and security incidents[20], there were several alarming statistics around the state of today's small businesses being able to protect their sensitive information. These issues paint a picture of the escalating threats that businesses face as many of their security programs and initiatives lag or are static at best.

- 52% of respondents reported they had experienced at least one ransomware attack, with over 79% stating that the ransomware was unleashed due to phishing or social engineering attacks.

- 54% of respondents reported that their breach involved sensitive information about customers, employees, or business plans, with the average breach now involving over 9,000 records.

---

[20] The 2018 State of SMB Cybersecurity, Ponemon Institute, 2018
   https://start.keeper.io/2018-ponemon-report

- Organizations continue to struggle to provide budget, technology, and personnel to manage security – 36% of respondents reported they are now outsourcing their IT security operations to outside partners.

- The toll of a cyberattack is becoming costlier. The impact to businesses due to damage/theft is averaging $1.2 million, and the disruption caused by a cyber-incident is also averaging $1.2 million. Examples of these costs include:

  ☐ The cost to forensically recover lost or damaged sensitive information;

  ☐ Liability costs to the business from lawsuits (customers, vendors, partners, etc.);

  ☐ The cost of fines due to not meeting compliance/regulation requirements or contractual requirements; and,

  ☐ The cost due to the loss of business opportunities from brand damage or loss of data, facilities, etc.

As small businesses face the shock of these threats to their operations, they must also be aware that consumers are now more concerned than ever about the security of their personal information. Every day, people are experiencing the effects of the hyper-connected society we live in. When they trade the data created about them as they search and transact online in exchange for services and discounts, consumers assume their information is being protected. SMBs and their security organizations must be cognizant that consumers are now willing to change their buying behavior and shift brands if they feel a business is at fault for a data breach of the personal information they have entrusted to the business. So even if you work for a small company, if you are believed to be at fault, you can expect brand damage and some level of impact on business operations.

To manage this impact, it is the SMB's security manager who is responsible for helping the business understand the convergence of data privacy and cybersecurity. There are several recommendations the security manager can incorporate to facilitate an understanding of how the company can manage its risk exposure and the sensitive data entrusted to the business.

Recommendation #1

How the SMB manages data privacy shouldn't be a secret – Customers need to understand why the business needs their information, how the company will use it, and for how long the company will retain it. Consumers are educating themselves about privacy, and they expect the SMB's policy on data privacy to be available and easy to read. The California Consumer Privacy Act (CCPA) and the European Union's General Data Protection Regulation (GDPR) require this level of transparency. Security managers will be expected to assist in creating this policy, helping the SMB select controls to protect the information, and leading the incident response team when there is a breach of this data. Because of this involvement, it is imperative that security managers understand which data privacy regulations pertain to their company and help devise the company's process for keeping that data private.

Recommendation #2

Data privacy is an "everyone initiative" – If the small business has sensitive information about employees, consumers, or partners, then you, as the security manager, should educate and train your whole company on how they can help protect this data. Incorporate a data governance program that uses training, processes, personnel, and technology to manage this information when it is at rest, in transit, being processed, and finally, destroyed when no longer required. All staff, partners, and vendors need to be involved and understand the importance of managing the sensitive data entrusted to the SMB, and they should be informed of the process for notifying the SMB and security manager about any possible breaches to this critical asset.

Recommendation #3

Data governance and the management of privacy is continuous – To effectively manage protected data, an SMB's security and risk management programs will need to leverage a blend of technologies, frameworks, processes, and personnel. With all of these resources, it is still a continuous lifecycle of monitoring, remediating, and improvement. To not shortchange themselves, SMBs and their security managers should assign resources to manage this risk and understand the value it provides to business operations by creating and sustaining a risk-aware culture.

Recommendation #4

Don't forget the small things – As the security manager, when you train your staff, build a security and risk management program that is flexible and incorporates new policies and procedures. Remember that data is like water and can easily slip out of an organization's control, so be willing to bring in a trusted partner for a risk assessment to check on how your data is being accessed. Areas you will want to verify include sensitive data being transferred to employees' smartphones and portable USB devices, and left on decommissioned copiers or legacy data storage units. Use this partner to review your security controls and verify that the data entrusted to your SMB is secure.

These recommendations are just some ideas for what small businesses can do to better manage their data privacy requirements. Data privacy is becoming more visible and is an international driving initiative with the current European Union's General Data Protection Regulation (GDPR) law and the State of California's California Consumer Privacy Act (CCPA). It is the aggregation of new threats, laws, and consumer activism that makes data privacy a strategic initiative for all businesses to adopt as part of their core strategic operations.

Chapter 8

Why Data Governance Should Be Corporate Policy

Data is like water, and as water is fundamental for life, so too is data an essential resource for business, whether it's an SMB or a global corporation. Data governance is the process that ensures this resource is protected and managed correctly, enabling security and risk leaders to meet their customers' (the business') expectations.

Everywhere today, on any available media, we hear reports of businesses that have suffered from devastating data breaches. A majority of these incidents involved customer data that was entrusted to them. These security events impacted the affected organizations in many ways, from executive leadership stepping down to impending class-action lawsuits or decreased revenue resulting from the loss of customer trust.

It's this picture of dismal customer privacy and the business world's lack of security controls for the data entrusted to them that leads me to recall a question I have heard many of my peers ask after hearing about the latest breach. "Why didn't they have a data governance program in place?" Though you are a security manager for an SMB, your company is not too small to ignore this issue. How are you managing this essential resource?

Data governance is a methodical process an SBM can implement to manage sensitive data and ensure that it meets specific standards and business rules before entering it into a data management system. Data governance encompasses people, processes, and technology, each connected as an essential program for different types of industries, especially those that must meet regulatory compliance guidelines such as finance, healthcare, or insurance. For companies in these industries to achieve compliance, they must demonstrate that they have formal data management processes in place (using the components above) to govern their data throughout its lifecycle.

Implementing data governance from a process perspective involves four steps: data stewardship, data classification, data quality, and data management. These steps include information on how an SMB would define the data types it owns; what data is considered critical to operations; how this data should be audited; and the process for how the data should be monitored, stored, moved, changed, accessed and secured. It's essential to recognize that data governance is an ongoing process that needs to be aligned with business operations and be flexible so it can grow with the organization as it matures.

Here are the four main components of a successful data governance program:

1. Data Stewardship

Data stewardship is the process of identifying and assigning roles and responsibilities for the SMB's data. This step is where the security manager can help the business to identify which employees or groups are creating sensitive data, which should have overall responsibility for this data, which employees or groups use this data, and how this sensitive data is routed through the business and potentially shared with third parties. The titles one typically assigns under this process are Data User, Data Owner, and Data Administrator.

2. Data Classification

This step is one of the most important for the SMB and one of the most time-consuming. During data classification, the security manager and business stakeholders will look at all of the data types the company has identified and categorize them into groups. These data groupings will have labels such as "Public," "Restricted," or "Confidential." With each label, there should be a description of the types of data that fall into that category and the security processes and controls that should be followed to manage and protect that specific data type. I have seen security managers create data matrices to be used as an aid for training employees on how they should protect the company's information. I recommend that the security manager includes stakeholders from the various business units of the company. Their insights will be needed in developing processes to protect corporate data that do not interfere with operations.

3. Data Quality

The next process of an SMB's data governance program will involve employees who are using company data for specific operations. Data quality is the process of measuring the reliability of current datasets to provide information that can be used to make organizational decisions. If employees input inaccurate data into business intelligence software, then the resulting datasets used for strategic planning can be skewed. As you can imagine, not getting this process right can significantly impact an SMB's ability to conduct business. Data quality is the one component of the data governance program that must be fully mapped, managed, and audited to verify that the resulting datasets are clean and accurate. For a security manager, I have seen this outsourced to a trusted third party to assist the SMB in verifying data quality. If you outsource this task, stay involved so you understand the process and the issues that may need to be remediated.

4. Data Management

The final process is where all the SMB's data governance efforts come together. Here is where the security manager and company leadership actively manage data governance efforts, and it involves the creation of data-flow architecture diagrams, security controls, and business processes to properly maintain the company's data from inception to retirement – a full lifecycle. During data management, the business will have data owners as members of long-term projects for the implementation of data portals or cloud technologies such as data markets or data lakes. This final process is to make business data usable in multiple formats and available to teams no matter their location. It is in this process that workflows for how data access will be mapped, implemented, and audited to verify data is protected with the right level of security. This process is why you and your team will need to be involved to ensure the data is protected with the right level of security.

In previous chapters, we discussed how companies should train their employees and make sure they understand that data privacy is an "every employee" initiative. For organizations to do this efficiently and continuously, they need to enforce data governance processes, and this begins with you, the security manager. In closing, remember data is like water, and as water is a fundamental resource for life, so data is an essential resource for an SMB. Data governance ensures this resource is protected and managed correctly, providing the security manager with a methodology to follow and a means to measure the maturity of data protection efforts.

Chapter 9

Five Stages to Establishing Your First Cybersecurity Program

With the continued rise in cybercrime and its devastating impact on companies, businesses are making a strategic decision to develop their first security program. For SMBs, this can be a daunting task requiring skills, experience, resources, and technologies they don't have. To focus on growing revenue and "keeping the lights on," many young companies have outsourced their information technology to managed service providers (MSPs). This outsourcing allows the SMB to focus critical resources on business operations while the trusted partner provides the required technology services.

Until recently, that has been the norm; however, MSPs are maturing. Many are now adding security services to their offerings and becoming managed security service providers (MSSPs). But even with the availability of these new MSSP service offerings, businesses must face another reality. They still need someone within their company to be responsible for managing security with third-party services. The requirements imposed by managing these services often require firms to establish their first enterprise security program. For those initiating this course of action for the first time, there are five steps that I would recommend organizations take to be successful.

1. Responsibility

In this beginning stage, businesses will need a person responsible for establishing the asset inventory program and periodically conducting ongoing asset audits. This same security professional will also complete a risk assessment of the current technology and application portfolios and develop a list of deficiencies that have been prioritized for mitigation based on the impact to business operations. When businesses are small, IT and security services will typically be managed by a handful of harried employees and a trusted MSP or MSSP will provide strategic support. However, when a company matures to be between 100 and 300 employees, management teams start having the "we need to have a security program" discussion.

In establishing a security program to lead the above processes and services, the most critical decision an organization will make is to hire someone with experience to take responsibility for and lead this program. Unfortunately, not having a security program manager can result in underfunded security programs that exist with no purpose or vision because the business may lack visibility into or understanding of the strategic value an organized security program delivers to the business. This significant risk is why companies need to select a security program manager and collaborate with him/her as partners to ensure that the security manager implements controls and processes that meet business requirements. This requirement for a security leader is spelled out in some compliance regulations such as HIPPA and NYSDFS. Having this experienced security leader will provide the company with a professional who can educate the organization on its current risk exposures and develop options to mitigate these issues with minimal resource requirements.

2. Inventory

During this stage, the security manager and company stakeholders will conduct a continuous process of developing and managing a database that lists the organization's IT-related assets. This inventory can include hardware (e.g., laptops, desktops, switches, access points, tablets, phones, and servers), applications, services, accounts, and anything else the IT or security teams feel they need to document for visibility into what is on the company's networks. To start this process, the business (IT and Security Managers) will typically conduct an inventory of the following:

- Employees and partners who access the network

- IT-related devices that access the network

- Current IT and cybersecurity applications that are installed on the devices and networks

- Any work processes/policies that are used to manage the IT assets and networks

As you can imagine, this is a mammoth task, and once this repository of data is collected, it needs to be continuously updated and managed for accuracy. Much of this data will also help the business create a configuration management database (CMDB) that is critical for the security manager and any planned security initiatives.

One of the last steps in this stage is assessing the current network and security architectures, work processes, and standing policies. Much of this data is collected while creating the inventory database. The benefit provided to the business is an insight into current "cyber hygiene," such as policies, controls, and procedures that will need to be upgraded. It also helps identify possible architectural changes that could reduce risk exposure. At the end of the inventory stage, the company should have an effective asset management program, an understanding of its current network and security infrastructure, along with insights about areas for improvement. With this stage complete, the information that has been gathered will be a critical input for the next step, which is doing a more formal risk assessment.

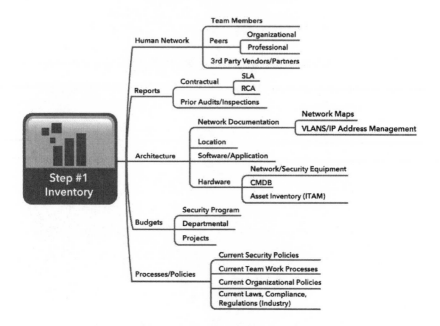

Step #1 Inventory

3. Assessment

In the previous stage, the business and its security manager gained critical visibility into its assets, but now it's time for everyone to get their hands dirty. The company needs to understand the risks associated with its current technology portfolio and business operations. The business gains this understanding through its security manager, who will use industry-accepted risk management frameworks such as NIST 800-53, ISO 27001:2013, or NIST 800-37 to document current security controls and highlight areas for remediation. Part of the operations in this assessment stage will involve the review and documentation of technologies and risk controls in the *security stack*. This includes technology such as firewalls, AV solutions, IDS/IPS sensors, and Security SaaS solutions. It also includes security procedures that are in place, such as patch management, incident response, and vulnerability scanning and remediation.

The newly upgraded network diagrams that the security and IT team created during the inventory stage will be useful here to help both IT and security personnel understand the current effectiveness of the implemented controls and note areas for improvement. Businesses and their security teams will find this stage to be the most technical of the five; they should not be afraid to ask third-party vendors to assist with these types of assessments and provide recommendations for improvement. By the end of the assessment phase, the SMB's security manager should possess a list of security gaps that will now need to be reviewed and prioritized based on business needs. Once completed, the results of this review will help the security manager develop their program's strategic plan. This process is discussed in the next phase, and stakeholders throughout the business must be

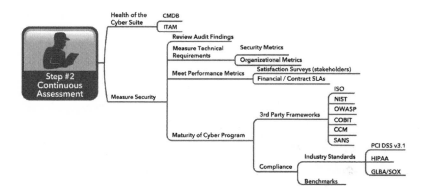

Step #2 Continuous Monitoring

included to help review assessment findings.

4. Prioritization

This final phase is where the business and its security manager will begin developing a strategic plan for security by first drafting the vision for upgrading the organization's current cybersecurity strategy (if one exists). The security manager will first review the current security program, and any currently identified challenges such as a lack of executive support, incomplete and inaccurate inventories (e.g., organizational blind spots related to hardware, software, and systems), previously identified audit gaps, and immature security processes. Once security leadership has completed this review, they will then invite stakeholders to be a part of reviewing the findings of the new assessment. Collectively they should prioritize findings based on the threat and risks to business operations, exposure to compliance requirements, and any possible unauthorized access to sensitive business data. With this prioritized list, the security manager will incorporate the results with their recent program review creating an updated security agenda. This updated security agenda should be used by the business to mature its strategic business plans and current budget proposals, helping the security manager prepare new initiatives to resolved identified security issues.

5. Cyber Hygiene

The repercussions of today's digital attacks (such as phishing emails and malware infections) on intertwined business infrastructures can result in loss of sensitive data and interruption of critical services to the SMB itself or to its customers. To counter these ever-evolving threats, companies, both small and large, need to focus on executing the necessary security processes and controls correctly and continuously. It's about businesses laying the equivalent of a digital foundation on which they can then build their networks and securely provide data and applications to their employees and customers. The methodologies businesses follow to perform basic security processes are referred to as "cyber hygiene."

Some services that are considered to be cyber hygiene include:

- Deploying and maintaining firewalls
- Updating anti-virus definitions

- Running vulnerability scans

- Selecting and maintaining identification and authorization mechanisms

- Updating and implementing software patches

- Backing up essential business data

- Securing personal data

Now understand, the previous list is not all-inclusive. Many services are considered to be cyber hygiene – it all depends on the business environment and the deployed technologies in use. It is essential for the SMB and its security manager to build a resilient security program by establishing a mature, continuous process of managing these services to reduce the organization's exposure to threats.

Security, when it is broken down into its basic components, is a discussion on risk management and the impact it has on business plans and operations. This risk is what drives companies, as they mature, to establish their first security program and hire a manager to lead them.

Chapter 10

Cyber Threat Intelligence (CTI): Providing Clarity to Cybersecurity Programs

Security managers and their security programs today often find themselves triaging a breach after the attack is over and analyzing digital artifacts as they try to piece together an event that happened in the past. Hopefully, the information they glean from the files, logs, and recovered data provides enough information to remediate any discovered security gaps and provide intelligence on possible future events. Unfortunately, as many security practitioners know, this can be a daunting effort where the adversaries that businesses face today are more agile and adept at making changes to sidestep attempts at stopping them. It's this untenable situation that drives organizations and security leaders to use strategic services such as cyber threat intelligence (CTI) to provide context about the adversaries that businesses face and the techniques, tools, and processes (TTPs) that are used against them.

CTI, as a strategic resource, revolves around three basic questions that security managers and their companies will need to address. The answers to these questions provide insight into why CTI is considered a valuable service when used correctly, and how businesses can be efficient in using this tool to mature their security program's management of ongoing and future threats.

1. What is cyber threat intelligence (CTI)?

This first question may seem pretty basic, but I have found many businesses and their security teams don't truly understand CTI or its value. In essence, CTI is a collection or grouping of information that is gathered from sources, human and electronic, both internal and external to the organization. This information is typically processed and evaluated to verify its validity. It is used to provide context about conditions necessary for a threat to exploit a vulnerability, and report whether threat actors are actively using the threat. Gartner defines threat intelligence as *"evidence-based knowledge, including context, mechanisms, indicators, implications and action-oriented advice about an existing or emerging menace or hazard to assets"*[21]. For those new to CTI, this means that for threat intelligence to apply to your organization, i.e., to have "context," there need to be deficiencies. Examples of deficiencies are such issues as immature security controls, unpatched or misconfigured hardware and software, or undocumented business processes. These deficiencies are what security professionals call vulnerabilities that can be targeted by cybercriminals for exploitation. It is the security manager's responsibility to understand these concerns, have visibility into the risk they place on their SMB, and through the use of strategic services, such as CTI, prioritize what needs to be remediated first.

2. Where can CTI be acquired?

For an SMB's security program to use CTI, they first need to make some decisions on what sources to use for their threat information. Keep in mind that even if you are a small business, threat intelligence can help the security manager make decisions to help the company be more resilient to security incidents. Just because you are small doesn't mean this is an asset you can't use to your benefit. The security manager has access to multiple sources of threat intelligence; these sources are categorized as follows:

a) *Internal threat intelligence* – information that is already within the business. This is information that a company's security and operations teams have from previous experiences with vulnerabilities, malware incidents, and data breaches. This

---

[21] *Definition: Threat Intelligence.* Retrieved from
   https://www.gartner.com/document/2487216

information, if properly documented, can provide the business with some meaningful content on how their enterprise networks were compromised and if any recurring malware or cyberattacks worked against the deployed security stack. This information, for most organizations, will probably reside in a log management system or SIEM platform. If this information on incidents can be collected and used to properly document a history of such things as attack paths, malware, and vulnerabilities, then it can provide invaluable insight into security gaps. These gaps can be remediated or help the company identify business processes or legacy issues that need to be addressed to prevent further compromises.

b) *External threat intelligence* – besides internal sources, organizations have the option to subscribe to multiple external CTI data sources. Some of these sources are from vendors and come in the guise of digital data feeds incorporated as a module or service directly into security endpoint solutions or deployed assets like firewalls and security gateways. Other sources will be in a report format, available through email or a CTI portal. This information provides the security manager and security team with an in-depth analysis of threat actors and their tactics, techniques, and procedures (TTP) that are currently targeting similar business operations or similar technology stacks. Some of these external threat intelligence feeds may be industry specific. One example is FS-ISAC[22], or as it is known in its full name the Financial Services Information Sharing and Analysis Center. It is an industry forum for collaboration on critical security threats that is used by the financial services sector. As a member of such a collaborative forum, the security manager could get alerts on current security issues, access to ongoing threat white papers, and access to peers who can speak about best practices to remediate identified concerns. Another external CTI source is provided by

---

[22] https://www.fsisac.com

law enforcement or government organizations. Some businesses may operate in industry verticals that are designated as critical infrastructure. With the critical infrastructure designation, security managers can request access to threat intelligence feeds and security services not ordinarily available to public companies – see DHS Enhanced Cybersecurity Services (ECS) for more information.

3. What are some use cases for why CTI is essential to SMBs?

After CTI sources have been selected, the focus now needs to be on the use cases for how this information can be leveraged to provide value and reduce risk exposure to the SMB.

a) *Improved Network Security Operations* – CTI can be used by the SMB's security manager and the security team to help improve the performance of the installed security stack. Next-generation firewalls, IDS/IPS systems, and secured web gateways are just some of the technologies that apply rules to block malicious traffic. CTI can be used to validate threat indicators, malware signatures, and domain reputations, and can help reduce false positives. Using streaming CTI as a service built into these devices, the business should be able to take advantage of near real-time threat analysis and threat reduction – basically, remove the noise so we can see the bad stuff.

b) *Patch Management Prioritization* – Patch management is one of the primary security controls used by all security programs, but it is never 100% effective. The process is time-consuming, and even when using patch management platforms that have been automated and tuned to their respective enterprise environments, a security manager will still need to prioritize which patches to apply. CTI can help patch management teams save time and be more efficient.

They help prioritize patches based on vulnerabilities that are being actively exploited and used to target similar businesses. This process saves the security manager from just relying on a CVSS score by adding some context on what threats are actually occurring, allowing them to focus resources on those prioritized vulnerabilities.

c) *Security Operations* – Most enterprise network environments generate more alerts than security operations center (SOC) teams or incident response (IR) teams can adequately investigate. Analysts triage this deluge of data into events that should be escalated to the IR team, activities to investigate when time permits, and events that look normal, to be ignored. In this environment, CTI can be used to provide situational awareness. Risk scores can be attached to threat indicators that will generate a flag in the security operation center's SIEM. This would alert analysts to query the threat database to investigate a high priority threat anomaly, allowing both teams more efficient use of their time and providing contextual threat data on the events they are investigating. This analysis would typically be beyond the security team of most SMBs; however, it may be a service offered by the SMB's managed security service provider (MSSP). Security managers should be familiar with this business case and request it if possible, to provide better tuning on anomalous data.

d) *Attack/Threat Analysis* – CTI for this use case can assist IR teams when they are responding to an active cyber incident. When the attack is initially detected, CTI can provide insight into who might be behind the attack, the tactics and tools used to initiate the attack, and the likely impact on the organization. I have used it during an incident response event to obtain real-time information on the type of attack we were seeing and to assist the triage team by providing recommended procedures to halt the incident and clean up its aftereffects.

e) *Triage and Remediation* – In this final use case, CTI is used by the IR teams and information security teams to uncover and document the impact of a breach event. Unfortunately, cybercriminals will conduct attacks in waves using multiple tools and techniques. I have seen attacks where several types of malware were used together, and by using CTI, my teams knew which indicators to look for as we searched through the debris left after the initial intrusion incident. Using CTI in this last case provides vital information to security teams so they can quickly search for and remove any attacker's residual connections from the network.

I hope from this discussion that I have provided some compelling points on why cyber threat intelligence should be used to improve security programs and provide valuable benefits to organizations' strategic business operations. I genuinely believe CTI is a strategic resource, and even though as a security manager you may serve an organization that is not mature enough for all of these business cases, it's still important to incorporate what you can and train your teams on how to efficiently use the selected information sources/tools for the benefit of the company.

Chapter 11

Establishing an Incident Management Process for SMBs

In today's dynamic threat environment, developing an approach to managing incidents is a strategic imperative for all companies, no matter their size or maturity. With that said, SMBs are a regular target of cybercriminals, and the impact of a cyberattack can be crippling for growing businesses that are tight on resources. The key action I believe SMBs should take in managing this risk is to be proactive and hire a security manager whose responsibility will be to establish – and practice – a security and incident management program that can train the business to prepare for the worst.

I'm a realist. I know this is easier said than done. Businesses, especially small businesses, are focused on revenue and implementing cybersecurity is hard to justify when your organization's priorities are to stay solvent and focus resources on critical operations. My counter to this argument is that companies and their security managers need to put a stake in the ground and start somewhere. Part of that starting process includes not only applying cyber-hygiene basics to help protect corporate assets, data, and employees but also establishing and training employees on how the business will manage its incidents.

Then, as an organization matures, the security manager can use the SMB's established incident management process as a foundation to grow its footprint. This maturing security and incident management initiative will serve as a core business resource to protect the growing company's new operations and ongoing strategic plans.

Starting with the basics for an SMB, I would recommend that the security manager use an established risk management framework as a template (roadmap) to begin creating the necessary cybersecurity policies, procedures, and programs. One framework I like to use is NIST's Cybersecurity Framework, which is centered on the five core functions of Identify, Protect, Detect, Respond, and Recover. I believe this approach to managing risk can also be used by a security manager to create a methodology for incident management that they are comfortable with.

The following are five core functions recommended by the NIST CSF; I have noted within each of them incident management processes that security managers can develop to help protect their organizations.

1. Identify

In this function, the business, led by its security manager, develops an understanding of its risk and then implements capabilities to manage it. Core tasks in the Identify function are orientated towards gaining an understanding of the critical systems, assets, data, and capabilities required for company operations.

- The security manager and business stakeholders identify and prioritize critical business systems and processes which may be exposed to compromise. Think of the procedures, applications, data, and people required for essential operations needed by the organization to function as a business.

- The security manager and business stakeholders, to include the SMBs leadership team, collaborate and develop disaster recovery and business continuity plans (DR/BC) while considering some or all of the following requirements:

  ☐ Coordinate how the business works with suppliers and primary customers during a business emergency.

☐ Plan how the business would conduct manual or alternative business operations if required.

☐ Plan how the company would do offline financial transactions.

☐ Develop written procedures for emergency system shutdown and restart.

☐ Develop and test methods for retrieving and restoring backup data; periodically test backup data to verify its validity.

☐ Have established agreements and procedures for conducting business operations in an alternate facility/site.

☐ Educate and train staff on the Business Operations Plan and DR/BC Plan.

2. Protect

As part of this phase, the SMB invests in a security manager and a cybersecurity program with appropriate security controls and capabilities. The core tasks in the Protect function are centered on the organization developing the strategic processes to limit and contain the impact of a cybersecurity incident.

- The security manager develops core critical "cyber hygiene" policies (Magazine, Security, 2016), including Acceptable Use, Access Control, Change Management, Information Security, Incident Response, Remote Access, BYOD, Email/Communication, and Social Media. These policies are reviewed and accepted by the business and then annually reviewed for updates.

- The security manager is charged to develop and implement an enterprise cybersecurity program comprised of at least these best practices:

☐ Backup business data (daily – incremental / weekly – full).

☐ Keep all systems updated with anti-virus and anti-malware security software.

☐ Keep all computers updated with current operating systems and security patches.

☐ Secure wireless networks with encryption and vendor-recommended security procedures.

☐ Implement, monitor, and audit system and network logging.

☐ Implement access control and authentication of critical/sensitive networks and business data.

☐ Train employees in cybersecurity awareness and proper use of business systems.

3. Detect

The security manager recommends, and the SMB approves the implementation of, appropriate security controls and technologies to identify and investigate the occurrence of a cybersecurity event. The core tasks in the Detect function are focused on the timely discovery and investigation of anomalies and abnormal events through continuous monitoring and detection.

● The security manager is tasked with implementing continuous assessment, monitoring, and remediation of network and other assets deemed critical to the business as part of the security program.

● The security manager reviews the skillsets and experience of their team and develops a training program for security personnel on the use of cyber threat intelligence and management of anomalous events.

● The security manager and business stakeholders collaborate and develop an incident response plan for the organization's cybersecurity teams to manage during a cyber event by doing the following:

☐ Maintain a current inventory of computer assets (hardware, software, and cloud).

☐ Maintain a list of IT service providers and emergency/law enforcement contact information.

☐ Create a checklist of specific actions in the event of a cyber incident.

☐ Define and establish priority notification to employees.

☐ Define and establish priority notification to customers and clients as deemed necessary and at the appropriate time.

☐ Define other notifications (e.g., law enforcement).

☐ Account for regulatory compliance (as required).

☐ Conduct refresher training on incident response emergency procedures (at least annually).

4. Respond

The security manager implements the appropriate controls and procedures to be activated in the event of a confirmed cybersecurity incident. The core tasks of the Respond function are designed to support the business' ability to contain the impact of a cybersecurity incident.

- The security manager, as the Incident response team leader, is tasked with identifying impacted or compromised systems and assessing the damage.

- The security manager, as the Incident response team leader, is tasked with implementing incident response plan actions (emergency or contingency plans) to minimize the impact on business operations.

- The security manager, as the incident response team leader, will direct incident response team members to preserve evidence of the incident while disconnecting or segregating affected identified assets.

- The security manager, as the incident response team leader, will direct incident response team members to collect the affected assets' system configuration, network, and intrusion detection logs.

- The security manager will notify appropriate internal parties, third-party vendors, and authorities, and request assistance if necessary.

- The security manager, as the incident response team leader, will direct incident response team members to reduce damage by removing (disconnecting) affected assets.

- The security manager, as the incident response team leader, will direct the incident response team scribe to document all steps that were taken during the incident.

- The security manager, as the incident response team leader, will conduct a "lessons learned" discussion to improve the incident response team's procedures.

5. Recover

The organization and its IT and security managers develop and implement procedures to be activated in the event of a cybersecurity incident. The core focus of the Recover function is to keep the company in operation during such an event and assist in recovery efforts as it returns to normal business operations.

- Restore recovered assets to a periodic "recovery point" if available and use backup data to restore systems to last known "good" status.

- Ensure all backups of critical assets are stored in a physically and environmentally secure location.

- Remember that updating recovered systems with current data may require the business to manually input transactions that were conducted offline due to a cyber event.

- Create an updated "clean" backup from the restored assets.

Re-establish full business operations when feasible and bring up all non-critical systems and operations.

For today's businesses, developing this risk management methodology is a strategic imperative for their continued operations. NIST's risk management functions are necessary steps an organization and its security manager can follow to reduce the impact of a cyber incident. It is important for an SMB to begin this process. Accept that it is needed and incorporate it into the business portfolio of critical operations that are required for the business to be successful.

Reading List for Section 3

1. *The 2018 State of SMB Cybersecurity*, Ponemon Institute, 2018
   https://start.keeper.io/2018-ponemon-report

2. *Data protection in the EU,* Eurpoean Commission, 2016
   https://ec.europa.eu/info/law/law-topic/data-protection/data-protection-eu_en

3. *California Consumer Protection Act (CCPA),* State of California Department of Justice
   https://oag.ca.gov/privacy/ccpa

4. *Security & Privacy Controls*, National Institute of Standards and Technology (NIST) Computer Science Resource Center, 2015
   https://csrc.nist.gov/publications/detail/sp/800-53/rev-4/final

5. *ISO/IEC 27001 Information Security Management*, ISO Standards:, 2013
   https://www.iso.org/isoiec-27001-information-security.html

6. *Risk Management Framework,* NIST Computer Security Resource Center, December 2018
   https://csrc.nist.gov/publications/detail/sp/800-37/rev-2/final

7. *Enhanced Cybersecurity Services (ECS),* Department of Homeland Security, 2019
   https://www.dhs.gov/cisa/enhanced-cybersecurity-services-ecs

8. *NIST Cybersecurity Framework,* NIST Computer Security Resource Center, 2019
   https://www.us-cert.gov/resources/cybersecurity-framework

9. FS_ISAC: https://www.fsisac.com

Section 4

Building Cyber-resilience

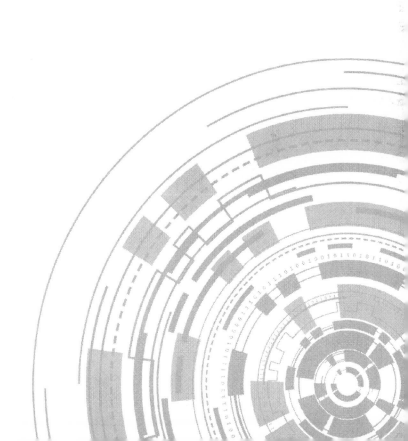

Now that you have the foundational elements in place, it's time to start adding value beyond the parochial expectations of your function. Chapter 12 helps you define the impact of cyber incidents on your organization and describes three programs, for cyber hygiene, training, and cyber insurance, to help you mitigate the impact of incidents.

Chapter 13 and Chapter 14 help you develop cyber-resilience, one of the most critical value adds you can provide. Chapter 13 helps you understand what resilience requires and Chapter 14 shows you how to incorporate resilience into your organization.

Section 4 ends with Chapter 15 providing a tutorial on security metrics to help you tell your value story.

Multiple resources on resilience are referenced in Chapter 13. The citations are provided as footnotes and links valid as of this publication date are provided in the curated reading list at the end of Section 4.

Chapter 12

Cyber Incidents and Their Impact on Small Businesses

In May of 2017, a leading security vendor surveyed over 600 IT decision-makers at medium size companies (100-499 employees) in three countries: the U.S., the U.K., and Australia[23]. The survey was focused on how these customers perceived new threats facing their organizations, were they prepared to manage incidents from these threats, and did they understand the costs to their organization if they had a cyber-related event. I'd like to review this survey and its startling results with you. I think the survey statistics are quite interesting and paint a picture that many SMBs may not fully understand the impact of an incident on their company's operations.

- 96% of those surveyed believe they are susceptible to cyber threats.

- 80% use a third party to assist the organization with security (mixed-use IT/security teams).

- 94% are making changes to their security budgets to account for mitigating new threats.

- 29% think they are ready to handle a cyber-related incident.

- 89% feel confident that they have the staff or resources that can manage a cyber incident when it happens.

---

[23] *The 2017 Webroot® Threat Report*
https://www-cdn.webroot.com/8114/8883/6877/Webroot_2017_Threat_Report_US.pdf

- 65% believe "brand damage" will be the hardest thing they will need to restore after an occurrence.

- Those surveyed believe the total cost, on average, for a breach of customer data records would cost the organization:

  ☐ $580,000 U.S.

  ☐ £738,000 U.K.

  ☐ AUD 1,893,000

As a security leader with over twenty years of experience, I look at these numbers and note several issues that concern me. I include this chapter to provide insight for the security professional charged to manage an SMB's security program. Traditionally, small businesses grow their IT departments slowly and do not have dedicated security staff. What I have found is that many of these growing companies typically assign security duties to one of their senior IT technicians, or they contract it out to an MSP. The reason for this is that cybersecurity is typically viewed as a resource that doesn't directly generate revenue or provide value to the business. Unfortunately, in today's business environment, if you connect to the internet, you are a target. It doesn't matter if you are a one-person home-based business or a medium-size business of 450 employees. Both companies are at risk; it's just a matter of scale. With that in mind, I think it's a good time to discuss the statistics I listed above and what I perceive from these numbers.

It is interesting that, across the board, almost all of those surveyed (96%) believe they are susceptible to today's cyber threats, and 94% are making changes to their security budgets to mitigate these endemic risks. I hope many are hiring their first security manager to build a security program. Included with this good news of increasing security budgets, over 80% of those surveyed stated they are using some third-party resources to enhance their company's cybersecurity initiatives. These numbers are on par with what I have seen across the industry; most organizations cannot field full cybersecurity, forensics, and incident response teams. This is why many organizations contract these services out to MSPs, who have the staff that can provide these critical services and assist the SMB's security manager and team. With many of those surveyed using their MSP partners to assist them in managing cybersecurity, I would expect to see 89% of them feeling confident they have the required resources to manage an incident; however, the next number shocks me. Only 29% of those same companies think they are ready for that incident. Why is that? These results tell me that many of these companies may have contracted out services to help them respond, but have they trained their staff?

As a small business, I believe it makes sense to contract security and incident response services to an MSP. However, an SMB's security manager and its leadership team are still responsible for how their company and their partners respond when there is a breach – you can't contract away your accountability for exercising "due care." Understand that as a security manager, pushing incident response to your MSP and then sitting back and watching the fire happen is not feasible. You and your company will still be held accountable, so work as a team and train together. These survey numbers indicate that many companies are paying for security resources but need to train to improve their confidence that they can triage a cyber incident successfully.

The second point from this survey that concerns me is that the estimated total costs those surveyed believe they will pay to resolve a data breach is pretty low. In 2019, the Ponemon Institute and IBM published their annual global analysis on the cost of a data breach[24]. This document estimated that the average price per compromised record is $150, the average size of a breach is about 25,000 records, the average time to identify you have a breach is 279 days, and the

---

[24] *2019 Cost of a Data Breach report,* IBM Security in Collaboration with Ponemon Institute, June 2015
https://www.ibm.com/security/data-breach

total cost on average for that breach to your business is $3.9 million. I doubt most SMBs have that available in their budgets. Please understand that these costs are based on myriad factors that impact the business, over and above the cost of a file. Some of these costs are as follows:

- Cost to notify all customers that their data was compromised

- Cost to hire a public relations team to assist with the emergency

- Cost to hire forensics services to understand how the incident happened, what was compromised, and what needs to be restored

- Cost to restore data and clean up the enterprise networks that have been breached

- Cost of legal services to deal with any lawsuits or government investigative actions

- Cost to the business in lost revenue due to reputation damage or loss of compliance certifications

- Costs can go on and on and on...

I mention these cost components because as a security manager for your small business, you should understand that your costs will vary from the industry average numbers. They are probably lower than what your business can expect. In the event of a compromise of your customers' data, and the potential that this will be reported in the media, security incidents can be very expensive. As you can imagine, the impact can be quite devastating to small businesses, even if you have cyber insurance. If the company is found at fault for not installing security controls or following best practices, don't expect that cyber insurance policy to pay for any damages – so be prepared. To help you get ready for that incident that inevitably will come, let's discuss some practices that you can champion to help your company reduce its risk. I believe three quick strategies can assist small businesses:

1. Cyber Hygiene

It is estimated that at least 80% of the risk facing your organization from cyber threats can be reduced if, as the security manager, you implement basic security controls correctly and continuously monitor them. What are the basics? Have anti-virus and anti-malware applications on all of your assets and make sure they are current. Make sure all corporate assets, applications, and operating systems are fully patched and apply critical patches promptly; the industry-standard is usually two to four weeks after issuance to allow for testing. Back up critical data and keep at least one copy offsite; be sure to test your backup restoration processes at least quarterly to verify that they work. Have a firewall for your network, segment your network to protect critical operations, and turn on the personal firewall software on your desktop computers. These are only some of the basic security controls; for additional resources, please consult the section 4 reading list.

2. Training

For small businesses to manage the impact of a cyber-attack successfully, for them to be resilient, the security manager, security team, stakeholders, and all employees need to train. I would recommend using a good threat intelligence feed to help prepare IT and security personnel on the threats facing the business and then have them periodically meet to go over the procedures for how an incident would be managed. The company needs to build "muscle memory" into its incident response team, even if this requirement has been contracted out to an MSP. If that is the case, the small business and its security leadership should still request training sessions to go over how its staff will support the MSP during a cyber incident to ensure that all stakeholders understand their roles.

3. Cyber Insurance

Finally, after a small business has assessed its risks and mitigated them as much as possible, I would then recommend looking at having a cyber insurance policy. As I mentioned before, a cyber insurance policy by itself won't save the day. Cyber insurance is a tool that should be coupled with a funded security program, security controls, and training to manage a company's risk. Please note that policies are typically different for each company because of the services they may require. One note that I would make to assist a business looking into this – the highest costs I have seen from experience for a business when responding to an incident are (1) notifying all affected customers and (2) the forensics/data recovery services. Both of these can be quite significant, which is why I recommend having this type of insurance to assist the business in recovering quickly from a cyber incident.

As we finish this quick discussion, I hope I have provided some value as you continue your security manager journey for your SMB. I believe this survey demonstrates that the technology world small businesses operate in today is dynamic and quickly changing. For small businesses to manage their risk in this environment, I recommend investing in security early, partnering with an MSP when needed, and hiring a security manager to lead the security efforts. I also highly recommend that small businesses train staff members to respond to an incident with their MSP partners and do the security basics correctly and continuously.

Chapter 13

What Does a Cyber-resilient Business Look Like?

Resiliency is not just for large organizations. SMBs should incorporate resiliency principles as a means of reducing risk. As a community, we continuously hear that all companies are experiencing a rise in the threats and attacks they face and that there are new evolving threats are out there waiting to strike. I don't believe in fear-mongering; however, keeping this sense of urgency in mind, I think it's essential for the security managers of SMBs to understand what resiliency looks like, how it can fit into their security program's strategic plan, and how it will change an SMBs security budget. As the security manager and company start to contemplate what processes may require resiliency, don't forget that it is also important to include methods for measuring high levels of resiliency. The end goal is to effectively blend resiliency into critical business operations and develop metrics that the SMB's security manager can use to measure what level of resiliency equates to measurable business value, justifying the expenditure of security department resources.

The dictionary definition of resilience is the "*capacity to recover quickly from difficulties.*" In cybersecurity, the definition of resiliency is focused on how organizations recover from an incident that incorporates multiple domains such as cybersecurity, business continuity, disaster recovery, and organizational operations. The *objective of cyber resiliency is for the SMB to be able to adapt and continue delivering services to its customers while the event is ongoing and being addressed by their security manager and team.* Additionally, the business operations domain should include processes to restore standard business services after the incident occurs.

From a security manager's perspective, I believe this concept is critical to protecting an organization's strategic operations. While I researched cyber resiliency for improving my organization's business continuity operations I enjoyed the work done by MITRE, which showcased their version of a Cyber Resiliency Engineering Framework for businesses[25]. They pictured a methodology of techniques that, when incorporated together, helped organizations meet specific objectives and enabled resilient business operations. Fast forward to 2018, and many of the same authors and researchers from MITRE matured their research, which is now available in the current NIST publication, *"Cyber Resiliency Considerations for the Engineering of Trustworthy Secure Systems."* It is absolutely worth reading.

For cyber resiliency, the NIST publication states that there are specific techniques that provide a level of trustworthiness when adequately incorporated into a business' security and risk management portfolio. I find that many of the methods listed by the new NIST cyber resiliency publication[26] can be traced to fundamental cyber hygiene principles. Note that we have covered many of these principles in chapter four, so if you were reading along and implementing them to help your SMB you were already incorporating resilient practices. – congratulations!

The following are the NIST resiliency techniques, with hygiene controls and practices in bold, that security managers for small businesses can implement to mature their security programs and improve their company's ability to provide services during a cyber incident. For an SMB, it may not be practical or within current resources to implement all of the listed security controls. If you are in this position, collaborate with a trusted MSP/MSSP to implement those that make sense for your business. Recommended techniques include:

---

[25] *Cyber Resiliency Engineering Framework,* MITRE, September 2011
[26] *Developing Cyber Resilient Systems, NIST* Computer Security Resource Center November 2019

Adaptive response

Optimize the ability to respond in a timely and appropriate manner to adverse conditions. With a current inventory, configuration management database (CDMB), and active monitoring, a security manager can actively triage a breach and remove or isolate compromised assets without having to bring business networks down.

Hygiene controls and practices to consider: Dynamic Reconfiguration, Resource Allocation & Adaptive Management.

Analytic monitoring

Maximize the ability to detect potential adverse conditions and reveal the extent of adverse conditions. These solutions provide the incident response team members with data in real-time so they can isolate and remediate anomalous issues without impacting business operations.

Hygiene controls and practices to consider: CDM, IDS, Threat Monitoring, Forensic & Malware Analysis.

Coordinated protection

Require an adversary to overcome multiple safeguards. The concept of layered security controls is that such an adversary may get in, but in the process of doing so makes enough noise and leaves enough digital tracks that they lose the advantage of being hidden.

Hygiene controls and practices to consider: Defense-in-Depth, Network/Host IDS, Orchestration, Red/Blue Team Exercises.

Deception

Mislead or confuse the adversary or hide critical assets from the adversary. Not all networks can remediate legacy technologies, nor can all companies afford security technologies. Deception is a strategy of layering multiple technologies so the adversary can't know which assets are real and which are decoys. Again, this process is designed so that cybercriminals make enough noise and leave enough digital tracks that they lose the advantage of being hidden.

Hygiene controls and practices to consider: Obfuscation, Encryption of Data, Honey Pots, Encrypt Processing, DNS Cache Poisoning.

Diversity

Limit the loss of critical functions due to the failure of replicated standard components. This is where SMBs and their security managers may select specific controls and build in redundancy, such as firewalls that operate in pairs or servers that work in clusters.

Hygiene controls and practices to consider: Different OS, Random IP space, Alternate Communication Protocols.

Dynamic positioning

Impede an adversary's ability to locate, eliminate, or corrupt mission or business assets. As they say, don't have all your critical assets in the same datacenter or S3 bucket. Segment operations so that even if a portion is offline due to a cyber-event, the business can still provide some essential services to its customers.

Hygiene controls and practices to consider: Relocate sensors, change storage sites, and distribute critical processes and assets.

Dynamic representation

Support situational awareness, reveal patterns or trends in adversary behavior.

Hygiene controls and practices to consider: Real-time map of resources, threat modeling, CTI for real-time awareness.

Non-persistence

Provide a means of curtailing an adversary's intrusion.

Hygiene controls and practices to consider: Employ time-based or inactivity-based session termination, refresh services, SDN.

Privilege restriction

Restrict privileges based on the attributes of users and system elements. One of the core security hygiene practices is to control employee accounts and account privileges, and auditing of how accounts are created or removed. Accounts are one of the processes most targeted by cybercriminals. Make the implementation of these controls a priority and continually monitor changes to access privileges.

Hygiene controls and practices to consider: Least Privilege, RBAC, Dynamic account provisioning.

Realignment

Reduce the attack surface of the defending organization. Limit the company's tech sprawl to only what it needs and transfer the risk to trusted vendors/partners.

Hygiene controls and practices to consider: Whitelisting, IAM, minimize non-security functionality, outsource non-essential services to an MSP/MSSP.

Redundancy

Reduce the consequences of loss of information or services. As the security manager for your company you should work with your peers and fellow business units to identify the critical assets that should be earmarked for backups or redundancy. Once in place, test backups to verify they work and will be ready when needed.

Hygiene controls and practices to consider: Retain configurations, maintain and protect backups, alternate audit and security capabilities.

Segmentation

Limit the set of possible targets to which malware can easily be propagated. Flat networks are evil. I know I am silly, but it doesn't do any good to put these other security controls in place if you leave the enterprise environment flat – it's wide open for compromise. Segment the network and limit the rights of employees so they can only access and see those segments needed for their job. Doing this limits the amount of intrusion a cybercriminal gets if they use a compromised account. It's another core security control – implement it and make it a standard procedure for the security and IT teams to follow.

Hygiene controls and practices to consider: Subnets, VLANs, Partitions, Sandboxes, Enclaves, System/Service/Process Isolation.

Substantiated integrity

Detect attempts by an adversary to deliver compromised data, software, or hardware, as well as successful modification or fabrication.

Hygiene controls and practices to consider: Tamper seals, cryptographic hashes, SCRM, Code signing, Trusted path, fault injection.

Unpredictability

Increase an adversary's uncertainty regarding the system protections which they may encounter.

Hygiene controls and practices to consider: Rotate roles, random authentication, randomize routine actions.

As a security manager reviewing these techniques, imagine an equation that demonstrates their business value to your organization: *Cyber Hygiene Controls + NIST Techniques = Objectives = Business Value through Resilient Operations.* For an SMB to meet the objectives for resiliency listed below, their security manager must follow a security framework, implement security controls (techniques) to manage business risk exposure, and continually monitor for changes in risk over time. This process is part of the roadmap security professionals use to mature their organization's security program. The techniques above and the following objectives provide the security manager with context for the value and impact proper security operations give the business. Objectives include the following:

1. *Prevent or Avoid* – Apply basic cyber hygiene and risk-tailored controls, decrease the adversary's perceived benefits, and modify configurations based on threat intelligence.
2. *Prepare* – Create and maintain cyber incident scenarios and train the incident response teams on the proper responses and procedures.
3. *Continue* – Minimize degradation of service delivery.
4. *Constrain* – Identify potential damage, change or remove resources and how they are used to limit future or further damage.
5. *Reconstitute* – Identify untrustworthy resources and damage, restore functionality, and determine the trustworthiness of restored or reconstructed resources.
6. *Understand* – Understand adversaries and understand the effectiveness of cybersecurity and controls supporting cyber resiliency.
7. *Transform* – Redefine mission/business functions to mitigate risks.
8. *Re-Architect* – Restructure systems or subsystems to reduce risks.

Cyber resiliency and its value to a company and its customers will depend on how well the SMB supports its security manager and incorporates the security program into its daily business operations. This partnership can begin small by focusing on fundamental cyber hygiene processes and techniques. Then over time, include and build redundancy into core business operations. Using the basics as a template, the security manager can implement more advanced resiliency techniques and, in the process, provide their SMB with the ability to deliver core services to customers even in times of adversity.

Chapter 14

Cyber-Resiliency – Simple Steps for SMBs

In May of 2018, I published an article in CSO magazine[27] in which I discussed with readers what a cyber-resilient business should look like and the techniques and best practices their security manager and the team would follow to protect business operations. In my article and in the previous chapter, I provided brief definitions of resiliency that are focused on an organization's ability to recover from an incident and how this critical business process would incorporate multiple domains such as cybersecurity, business continuity, and disaster recovery. As I mentioned in Chapter 6, the concept of businesses being resilient has recently come into focus and become a significant question for many companies due to the growing complexity of threats and vulnerabilities they face. I had proposed in both my article and Chapter 6 that a good visual cue for security managers to use to help their organizations understand how they can be resilient would be:

Cyber Hygiene Controls + NIST Resiliency Techniques = Objectives = Business Value through Resilient Operations

To summarize, for a business to meet the objective of resilient activities, it needs to hire a security professional to manage security efforts. This includes incorporating a security and risk management program, implementing security controls (including security techniques) to manage its risk exposure, and continually monitoring for changes in risk over time. So, with this context in mind, and

---

[27] *Cyber-resilient, Hayslip, Gary May 2018.*
  https://www.csoonline.com/article/3273346/what-should-a-cyber-resilient-business-look-like.html

thinking about both small and medium size businesses (SMBs), the purpose of this chapter is to answer this recurring question, "Thank you for the information on resiliency, but where should our security team start?"

In cybersecurity, one of the most fundamental requirements for security professionals is visibility. If the security manager or security team can't see it, and if the CISO and security team doesn't know the asset or service exists, then how can they understand its potential risk and protect their company from its exposure? It's this context that led me to write about cybersecurity as a lifecycle, a process of continuous interlinked operations. The first step in the cybersecurity lifecycle was "Inventory," which I believe applies to our current discussion on cyber-resiliency. For an SMB to begin its effort to become cyber resilient, the security team must have continuous, accurate visibility. For an SMB's security manager and team to have visibility, they must know what is essential to the business and what resources are required to protect and provide business operations during an incident. That leads us to our first step, which begins with executive leadership:

Step 1: Who are we? What is our purpose?

The importance of this first step can't be overemphasized. You will find I will continually mention "Inventory" and discuss how this continuous process feeds many of the simple operations and security controls that are baseline requirements for a security manager and their team. Let's start with a hard question. Do the leaders of the company genuinely understand not just their business operations and the products they produce, but also the critical resources they will need for them? This is not a trick question. I have found numerous times that when asked, very few managers or business executives have the complete picture. Having this full picture is critical during an emergency and can provide the security manager with the context required to isolate a data breach with minimal impact on possibly vital business services. This step should not include collecting documents such as previous audits, budgets, and network maps. This facet of inventory will involve discussions between the security team, key stakeholders, business unit leaders, and executive leadership. These meetings are to document the vital resources, equipment, and services, and the types of data the business creates, processes, and shares with its partners. Answers to these questions will provide the SMB, its security team, and stakeholders with insight into the core processes needed for business and the types of data they have and who they share it with, which may have specific compliance requirements during a data breach. All of the information collected during the inventory phase should be verified, protected, and continuously updated for use by the SMB's security team for risk management purposes, or provided to a third party MSSP for tailored risk mitigation services.

Step 2: What resources and risks do we currently have?

Once an SMB and its security team have the initial inventory of critical operations, services, assets, and data types documented, the security manager must now review what resources they currently have available to keep this information current and protect it from compromise. In this step, the security manager is conducting an audit of the current resources used for security, to include internal SMB-owned assets and any contracted external services. In this step, the SMB's leadership should work with their security manager to review the previous list of critical operations and discuss any recommendations for improvement, such as how resources may need to be reallocated to manage security operations better. In these discussions, the SMB's leadership team and its security manager need to review how they are identifying their current risks, which risks can be mitigated, and who has the authority to accept any outstanding risk exposure for the business. What is essential is that by the end of this step, the SMB leadership and its security team should understand how the business risk will be managed and if the current security program and its operations are adequately staffed and funded.

Step 3: Just how prepared are we?

By this step in the cyber-resilient process, the SMB's leadership team and its security manager have identified critical assets and current risk management processes, and documented the resources it has allocated for security operations. With this contextual information, it's now time to ask some hard questions. The SMB leadership team needs to review what types of risks (e.g., financial, competitive, operational, reputational, and regulatory) the company faces, and whether they have the mechanisms in place to deal with them effectively. The executive team needs to review what external partners they are connected to and what agreements are in place to safeguard the business in case of an external partner's data breach. It is during this stage that security managers will begin reviewing what incident response processes will fit their SMB's needs. Some questions the security manager must understand are:

- Does the company have current policies in place for disaster recovery and business continuity, and how do they factor in the case of a cyber-attack?

- Have these policies been tested, and if so, how often?

By the end of this step, the SMB leadership team and its security manager should understand the varying types of risks associated with company operations; they should know who their external partners are and what documentation is in place to reduce liability from them. The security manager should have also reviewed company procedures that concern cyber incidents and have documented a separate incident response process for the security team to manage its responsibilities during a cyber incident.

Step 4: Not all security is created equal.

With assets, risks, procedures, resources, and partners identified, our discussion for this chapter now focuses on one of the most critical aspects of preparing for resilient operations. This next step is for the leadership team and stakeholders to meet with their security manager and review the company's security program. The security program and its manager should have taken much of the previous information and incorporated it into security controls and processes to manage risk and add secondary resources for emergency operations. During this security review, the SMB leadership team needs to work with its security program manager and review the company's current security plans and the maturity of its overall program. During this review, it should be noted whether the policies cover both internal and external business operations. All policies, procedures, and workflows should also be reviewed to verify whether they include new services that are now cloud-based. This part of the process for incorporating resiliency allows the business to understand how well the security program has critical assets and services identified, and it provides an opportunity for leadership and their security manager to discuss any gaps that need to be addressed.

Step 5: Creating an action plan.

In this final step of the resiliency process, the SMB's leadership team and its security manager should now have a list of any immature processes or security gaps. It is in this stage that both incumbents should include stakeholders to review and prioritize this list of issues to align it to business operations. Developing issues should be identified for immediate action, and both short-term and long-term plans should be created for the security program to manage. This prioritized list can be used as a strategic plan by the SMB's security manager to establish the SMB's first risk baseline, and over time monitor reduction in risk exposure as the list's identified issues are mitigated. I have found from personal experience that the management of this plan should be periodically reported to leadership, and it will be a living document that will be adjusted over time as the SMB and its security program mature.

SMBs following the five steps above will be better prepared for the day they do have a cyber incident because they will know their risk exposures, and their security manager will be ready to respond to the emergency. The SMB's security teams and MSSP partners will have a better understanding of what assets and operations are critical to the business and will have tailored incident response plans to reduce the impact of any successful breaches. This chapter is by no means a complete guide for how SMBs can be resilient. I believe it is a starting point for how they and their security programs can make this a continuous process to be better prepared. Some resources I would recommend to assist SMBs and their security teams as they begin incorporating how they will manage their resiliency issues are provided in the reading list for Section 4.

Chapter 15

Security Metrics: Telling Your Value Story

As the security manager for an SMB, this chapter provides insight on how metrics are critical tools to be used by you and your program to explain how security services support the organization and its strategic objectives. Today, we witness an increasing number of cyber incidents across all industries. Boards of directors and senior management are educating themselves on their company's risk exposure to these cyber-related issues. Boards also are seeking a better understanding of the potential for cybersecurity initiatives to enhance their company's strategic operations. Many board members have questions for their security manager and staff, such as, "How secure are we from a particular threat?" or "Can you promise me we won't be the next [hacked company]?" Security professionals such as yourself need to be able to answer these questions and help board members understand that cybersecurity does not control the threat landscape facing the company but rather how the organization responds to these threats. The purpose of a mature cybersecurity program is to provide the business with a platform to manage its risk environment so these threats don't overwhelm the company.

An SMB's senior management team is often responsible for the development of a clear, concise strategy to address threats and vulnerabilities to cyberattacks. The security manager is expected to have technologies and security controls in place that reduce the organization's risk, as well as processes to monitor the overall effectiveness of the security program. It is standard best practice to use a risk management framework, such as NIST RMF, ISO 27001, or COBIT 5, as a platform or roadmap to establish the company's current risk baseline. With this framework in place, the security manager and team can select specific metrics as real-time input to provide visibility into the value security provides the business.

As a security leader, you must understand and embrace metrics as critical tools to tell the value story of your security program. There is no specific template for what should be measured with metrics; every company's business environment is different. I would recommend, however, that metrics be reported to senior leadership in the guise of a narrative, using the metrics to explain how the security services support the business and its strategic objectives.

Some primary considerations for creating this story with metrics are as follows:

1. **What is its purpose?** Metrics that you select should support a business goal. Connecting metrics to the business will help prioritize resources more efficiently.

2. **Is it controllable?** For metrics to have worth, they must demonstrate that specific goals are being met. So, metrics should measure processes and outcomes that the security team controls.

3. **What is the context?** Don't take the results of a security tool and call it a metric; it must have a purpose that will drive an action. Ask questions such as, "Why are we collecting it? What story does it tell?" Is the tool reducing risk or providing a new service that helps another business unit improve, and is that improvement measurable? That's a value story that explains why resources are needed and the benefit they provide the business.

4. **Is there an understanding of what "good" is?** You should know the target value you want to achieve and the actions you want to take (and resources required) based on that objective.

5. **Is it quantitative?** A quantitative value can be compared and demonstrate trends. Qualitative results are all right, but in all my years as a CISO, I have never used them before a board because they are extremely hard to rely on to make a point

about a subject. So keep them quantitative; believe me, it pays dividends for getting resources for new initiatives.

6. **How accurate is your data?** The data used to create a metric should have a high level of accuracy, precision, and reliability.

7. **Is it easy to process and analyze?** The data should be collected, processed, and posted to a central dissemination point. It should not take a long time to prepare and report your metrics. For example, if metrics are used in a weekly report, it should take two to three days to collect, process, and post the results.

The above recommendations help security leaders identify data and services to build the metrics they require. It is important to remember that the regulatory environment will influence what data you designate for collection to create your security and risk metrics. This applies even to small businesses. These metrics will also be dependent on the technologies deployed as part of the security stack, current security controls implemented within the business, and security services provided to the SMB by trusted third parties.

A good example of performance-based metrics is "Reduce desktop remediation time from six hours to four hours by <date>." Another metric that could be used to measure the number of servers needing critical patches is "Improve the number of fully patched servers from <current %> to 90% by <date>." What is important with both examples is you have a specific action you want to measure, you have something to measure it against, and you have a timeframe to demonstrate success. These examples are measurements that would be collected and imported into a data portal or dashboard to be analyzed and monitored for trends.

Now let's look at an example of how metrics can be used to provide insight into how well an SMB's security program is performing. A security manager may collect a metric to track the number of desktops compromised each month, but that in itself provides little value to the business. If that security manager had asked to invest part of their security budget in a new AV/EDR solution, how would they measure the value this solution provides the business and its effectiveness in reducing risk?

One way would be to estimate the cost of a compromised desktop. An infected desktop is removed, reimaged, and the employee's data is recovered from the previous night's backup. This process is equivalent to five hours of labor from the IT technician and five hours of lost productivity from the affected employee. Let's say the cost to the business is a combined $225 per infected desktop. Currently, the organization is averaging 45 infected assets per month, which is equal to $10,125 per month or an annual cost to the business of $121,500 in lost productivity. With the new AV/EDR solution installed, the number of infected desktops per month is reduced by 60 percent over time. This reduction in the number of infected assets and the savings to the business in lost productivity is a metric the security manager can use to educate the business on the value the company receives from its recent investment in this new technology.

As we finish our discussion, it's important to remember that security leaders will experience scrutiny from their businesses on the services provided by the security program. They will at times be required to meet with their SMB's leadership team or board of directors and demonstrate that they are good stewards of the resources provided to them as security manager. To adequately respond to these requests, the security manager can balance the efficiency and effectiveness of their selected security controls by understanding the metrics and data that must be collected to tell their security program's value story to the business.

To help with this process, two excellent sources to assist in creating metrics come from SANS[28] and the Center for Internet Security[29]. I am going to repeat this one more time because it is critical for you as

---

[28] *Gathering Security Metrics.* SANS Information Security Reading Room, 2009
[29] *CIS Benchmarks.* Center For Internet Security, 2019

a security manager: metrics are an asset that you can use to tell a story about the value your security program provides the business. Metrics are your opportunity to demonstrate how mature your security program is at risk-reduction and how you have built your SMB a business-enablement platform, so use them wisely.

Reading List for Section 4

1. *The 2017 Webroot® Threat Report*
   https://www-cdn.webroot.com/8114/8883/6877/
   Webroot_2017_Threat_Report_US.pdf

2. *2019 Cost of a Data Breach Report,* IBM Security in Collaboration with Ponemon Institute, June 2015
   https://www.ibm.com/security/data-breach?

3. US CERT (Cybersecurity and Infrastructure Security Agency) lists resources that support small businesses in recognizing their cybersecurity risks
   https://www.us-cert.gov/resources/smb

4. US Federal Trade Commission (FTC) provides a list of 10 practical lessons for small businesses called: *Start with Security: A Guide for Business.* US Federal Trade Commission, 2019
   https://www.ftc.gov/tips-advice/business-center/guidance/start-security-guide-business

5. *Cyber Resiliency Engineering Framework,* MITRE, September 2011 https://www.mitre.org/sites/default/files/pdf/11_4436.pdf

6. *Cyber Resiliency Considerations for the Engineering of Trustworthy Secure Systems,* NIST March 2018
   https://csrc.nist.gov/publications/detail/sp/800-160/vol-2/archive/2018-03-21

7. *Developing Cyber Resilient Systems,* National Institute of Standards and Technology (NIST) Computer Security Resource Center November 2019
   https://csrc.nist.gov/publications/detail/sp/800-160/vol-2/final

8. *Cyber-resilient,* CSO Magazine, Hayslip, Gary, May 2018
   https://www.csoonline.com/article/3273346/what-should-a-cyber-resilient-business-look-like.html

9. *Cybersecurity Essentials*, Cybersecurity and Infrastructure Security Agency
https://www.cisa.gov/cyber-essentials

10. *US-Cert Resources for Businesses*, Cybersecurity and Infrastructure Security Agency Resources for Business, 2019
https://www.us-cert.gov/resources/business

11. Start with Security: A guide for Business, Federal Trade Commission, 2019
https://www.ftc.gov/tips-advice/business-center/guidance/start-security-guide-business

12. *Geographically specific security resources for businesses*, Cybersecurity and Infrastructure Security Agency, 2019
https://www.us-cert.gov/resources/sltt#geo

13. *Gathering Security Metrics.* SANS Information Security Reading Room, 2009:
https://www.sans.org/reading-room/whitepapers/leadership/gathering-security-metrics-reaping-rewards-33234

14. *CIS Benchmarks,* Center for Internet Security, 2019
from https://learn.cisecurity.org/benchmarks

Risk Management

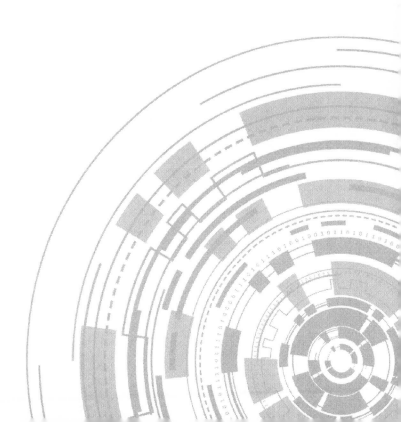

After developing the tactical programs for improving your cyber-resilience, it is now time to elevate the focus to the more strategic program of risk management. Cyber risk is only one element of enterprise risk but in small businesses, cyber professionals are often the most equipped to help the enterprise with overall risk management.

To help equip you for this role, Chapter 16 dives into risk management as an ecosystem. Chapters 17 and 18 then look at risk from the perspective of integrating with potentially one of your most important third-party relationships, the Managed Service Provider (MSP).

Section 5 also concludes with a curated reading list.

Chapter 16

Risk Management for the SMB: An Evolving Ecosystem

Over the last several years, I have written and spoken about how I view cybersecurity as a "continuous" lifecycle. I first conveyed this concept when I was the CISO for the City of San Diego, and at a local tech event my boss, the Mayor of San Diego, asked me the question most CISOs hate to answer. He asked me if our networks were secure. To a CISO, that is a loaded question because technology changes, threats continually change, and employees are in a constant state of change. After thinking to myself that this may be a resume-generating event, I answered him, "It's a work in progress." My answer, and the shock it induced, provided me with the opportunity to describe to the mayor the concept that cybersecurity is not just technology but a combination of technology, security controls, processes, and people, and this intertwined entity is a "continuous" lifecycle. In that discussion, I outlined to him how this lifecycle concept is used by cybersecurity professionals to provide insight to their organization's leadership on how the business security program provides value.

It has been several years since that evening discussion, and I have now come to realize that the concept of cybersecurity as a continuous lifecycle is limited in scope; it only addresses an organization's cybersecurity program from a daily "operations" perspective. In truth, an organization's cybersecurity program and its lifecycle are part of a broader ecosystem. This security ecosystem includes the cybersecurity lifecycle, the risk management lifecycle, and the dynamic interaction between their components and processes. This unique ecosystem, when documented and adequately maintained, provides an organization's leadership team with invaluable intelligence on the maturity of its cybersecurity and risk management initiatives and the resources being provided to manage them. It is the second half of this ecosystem, the management of enterprise risk, that I want to describe now and explain how I believe it can enhance the supervision of a cybersecurity program.

This chapter is included in this book to provide you, as the senior security executive for your small business, with insight into this continuous lifecycle that revolves around your program. As a security manager, it's your responsibility to understand the full scope of this ecosystem, manage it, and through experience, leverage it to protect your company.

Cybersecurity & Risk Management – The Ecosystem

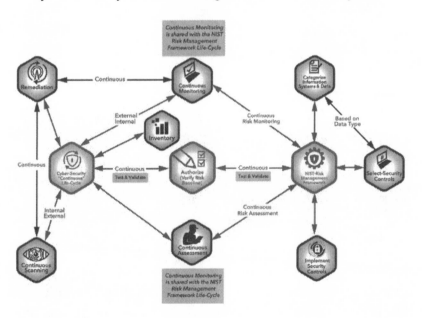

As I previously stated, the full security ecosystem includes the cybersecurity program, with all of its components, along with enterprise risk management. As the image above indicates, both cybersecurity and risk are intertwined, with the "Authorize" component shown in the middle as the linkage between both programs, used to continually test and validate selected security/risk controls, security/risk assessments, and risk monitoring results. For our discussion, I have chosen NIST's Risk Management Framework[30] to discuss an approach to enhancing your efforts as the security manager for your SMB. Keep in mind there are other risk management methodologies such as ISACA's COBIT 5 framework[31]; however, for this chapter and our discussion together, I will use NIST. I have used the NIST frameworks and policies in multiple CISO roles over the years to manage risk, and I believe they will be a solid frame of reference to help you learn several critical concepts.

Through this chapter, I hope to impart the strategic value that risk management will provide you and your small business; because even SMBs need risk management if they expect to survive in today's threat environment. As a security leader, gaining a better understanding of these lifecycles and how they combine as an ecosystem will help you reduce your organization's risk exposure and make you a more well-rounded business executive and partner.

Risk Management – A Lifecycle

The definition of risk management is the process of managing risk to an organization's business operations, assets, and/or personnel. This process involves identifying and analyzing risk, assessing recommended controls, implementing and validating selected controls, and finally monitoring for residual risk exposure. The Risk Management Framework from the above NIST RMF publication incorporates six steps to infuse a focused risk management process (lifecycle) into a business's strategic operations. These six steps are as follows:

---

[30] See reading list for Section 3
[31] COBIT 5, ISACA 2019 https://cobitonline.isaca.org/about

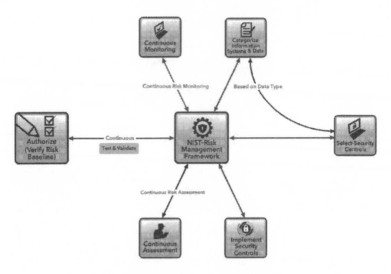

Risk Management Lifecycle

1. Categorize information systems and data

2. Select security controls

3. Implement security controls

4. Continually assess security controls

5. Authorize (verify risk baseline)

6. Continually monitor security controls

1. Categorize (Information Systems & Data)

This is the first of six steps in the risk management lifecycle. It involves understanding the threats and vulnerabilities facing SMBs' enterprise networks and the impact of these threats to corporate assets and operations. To do this effectively, security managers must know what IT assets (applications, servers, IT infrastructure, and networks) are their responsibility and how the business and its partners use these assets. As the security manager, you will find that to gain insight into these critical systems and their data, an understanding of the organization's data flows and processes is required. To assist the security manager in achieving this understanding, I would recommend that you:

- Document organizational data flows.

  ☐ Data flows and processes generated by current applications, services, and hardware

  ☐ Current network maps

  ☐ Application/hardware portfolios

- Speak with employees and partners – How is organizational data being used?

- Review how assets, employees, partners, vendors, etc. process corporate data.

- Is data backed up? Where is data stored? How is it protected?

- If data is transmitted out of the organization, do we know why and to whom?

The knowledge gained about the company's networks, applications, and the criticality of its data types will directly impact the next step – selecting security controls.

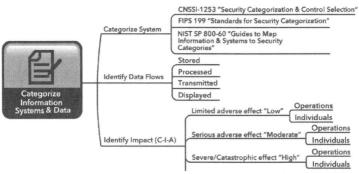

Categorize Information Systems and Data

2. Select (Security Controls)

In "Select," the knowledge acquired in "Categorize" is used as a template to select the appropriate security controls for protecting the SMB's IT and business assets. Note, the level and breadth of these security controls will be based on the data types and compliance requirements the security manager finds in their company. As a refresher, there are several control types that the security manager should be aware of, such as:

- Managerial Security Controls – Controls used in developing policy and procedures, measuring actual performance, ensuring compliance, and taking corrective action.

- Technical Security Controls – User authentication (login), logical access controls, antivirus software, firewalls, and other technology solutions.

- Operational Security Controls – Developing operational workflows and procedures, incident response processes, management oversight, security awareness, and training.

- Supplemental Security Controls (countermeasures) – These are compensating controls that are implemented when your organization cannot meet a requirement explicitly as stated.

After the required security controls have been identified, based on data types and compliance requirements, the security manager will then need to assess for security gaps, or as I like to say, "opportunities," that need to be remediated. As opportunities are identified, the security manager will be required to add supplemental controls to resolve them. Remember, as the security manager, you will weave these additional controls into the standing security framework and tune (adjust) them to the organization's business requirements. Controls impact business operations, so selecting the correct controls and adjusting them is extremely important.

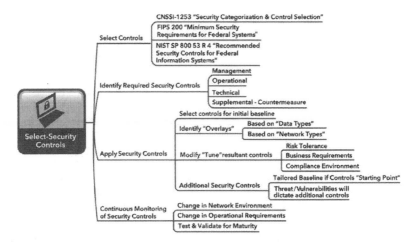

Select Security Controls

Another point to remember is that these same business requirements may require you to either relax a security control or add more stringent controls. This point is critical; the security manager must understand how stakeholders use business enterprise assets. This insight will help in selecting the correct compensating controls that provide minimal impact to operations. One final point is that when you "Authorize", you will revisit this "Select" step continuously to test and validate current controls. So, you must know your enterprise networks, its data, and how the company uses them.

3. Implement (Security Controls)

In this step, it's time to fully implement the security controls that you have "Selected" for your SMB's enterprise systems based on the company's compliance requirements and associated data types. Remember that security controls come in many flavors, such as updating a legacy workflow practice, installing new hardware technologies, or updating current software solutions. During this "Implement" phase, the security manager should review any newly selected technologies to verify they have been tested and validated by industry. This doesn't prevent the security manager from leveraging open source tools. However, if open source solutions are on the agenda, there are some important things to verify:

- The selected open-source solution has a community that supports the tool, and the FAQs/Support pages are current.

- The SMB's security staff have the skillsets to properly implement and maintain the open-source solution (no orphan apps/solutions allowed).

- The security and authenticity of the DLLs associated with the code (are there back doors?).

- Licensing requirements and the potential challenges with derivative works.

With security controls in mind, I believe I would be remiss if I didn't mention that it's best to research, document, and follow industry best practices and recommended vendor settings for the new security controls. After the security controls have been installed, tested, and are operational, it's then time to "tune" them to the business environment. Security managers should take this stage seriously and do as much research as required to understand the control and possible issues the security team may see once the control is operational.

At this "tuning" stage of the process, I have seen mistakes made that could have directly impacted an organization's ability to stay in business. Many of these mistakes were due to misunderstandings about how enterprise assets, data, or specific work processes were used in critical business operations. These types of misunderstandings can lead to controls being installed incorrectly, which in turn can limit an SMB's ability to be competitive or may open the company to new risk exposures that are beyond its ability to manage in the case of a security breach. These limitations and their impacts are why it is imperative that security managers talk with their peers in the business and other critical stakeholders to ensure they understand from their company's perspective which data and technologies are vital.

Again, this knowledge will assist the security manager and their team in tuning security controls correctly the first time, so they don't interfere with business initiatives. I know I am repetitive here. But when security breaks things in the business, you, as the lead security executive, lose credibility with the company's leadership team, which in turn makes it harder for you to do your job.

As you finish this step, document the current security controls and their new settings. Not only should the security team record these settings, but they should also include any new scan/test results in the security stack documentation so that team personnel have examples of what new outputs the matured security controls create. Remember, document now so you don't regret it later. Be aware that over time, security controls that burden your stakeholders will become worthless. Your stakeholders will find workarounds to bypass the controls, and the result is more risk exposure to your organization. Research them, understand them, tune them, and continually manage. This leads us to our next step.

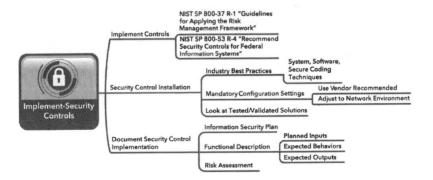

Implement Security Controls

4. Continually Assess (Security Controls)

This step of enterprise risk management is also present in the cybersecurity lifecycle. In continuous assessment, you will review the latest audit findings, new technical requirements, and all reported metrics for the company's current security stack. This part of the lifecycle is where the security manager will use the risk management framework to document new assessment findings and establish the SMB's current risk baseline. This baseline will be continually reviewed and should be used to identify the business's overall risk exposure and help facilitate discussions on how much risk the company is willing to accept. You will use this baseline in the next step, "Authorize," to periodically verify the validity of selected security controls and the environment in which they operate.

At the beginning of any new assessment, I would recommend that you meet quarterly with your team, stakeholders, and partners to review old assessment findings and discuss your security program services. You want to verify with your team and other stakeholders that the enterprise security suite is meeting expectations and providing strategic value to the organization. These periodic meetings should also include initiating and reviewing executive reports, SEIM logs, and collected metrics data if required. I would recommend that in these meetings you review the selected information and look for any trends that might be indicative of an immature process or a security incident. As you meet with your team and stakeholders, I would also recommend you ask if there are additions or modifications to the security portfolio that can be made to reduce risk or provide better services to the business. I have found from experience that during these discussions that you will gain insight into the maturity of your program from another's point of view, which will prove invaluable as you identify areas that need improvement.

After these meetings, I would recommend that you next review and document any recent changes to the currently selected security frameworks (CIS 20, ISO 27002, and NIST SP 800-53d). The findings from these frameworks provide the security program with references to measure and baseline its growth. What framework you select will be driven by the business environment your organization operates in, contractual obligations from selected vendors or trusted partners, and the types of data (data categories are fundamental) it processes, stores, and transmits. This step is also where the security team should research and document any contractual requirements or industry/regulatory compliance requirements that may apply to the business and influence the security program and its operations. These regulatory frameworks typically apply to the business because the company is creating, processing, or storing some protected data or the company operates in a regulated business environment.

Compliance standards such as PCI[32], HIPAA[33], SOC-2™[34], and CCPA[35] are very similar to the security frameworks (e.g., NIST, COBIT, or ISO). However, compliance standards, even though they may require security controls like a framework, have substantial penalties and fines associated with them if the organization fails an audit. I would recommend that you, as the security team leader,

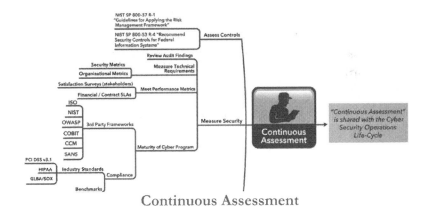

Continuous Assessment

---

[32] *Payment Card Industry Data Security Standard* (PCI-DSS), PCI Council, 2018

[33] *Health Information Protection and Accountability Act* (HIPAA), HHS, 2019

[34] *Service Organization Controls Type 2* (SOC-2™) for Service Organizations, AICPA 2019

[35] See reading list for Section 3

create a data repository or portal to track your company's compliance documentation. As part of this step, periodically review any controls that have findings, manage the remediation of these findings, and document them to resolution. This step is all about continually reviewing the security program, risk management program, and asking questions. If in doubt, document it!

5. Authorize (Risk Baseline)

In this step, I am going to deviate from the NIST Risk Management Framework (RMF) guidelines. If an organization is part of the Federal Government or does business with the Federal Government, you follow NIST RMF. The "Authorize" process is your formal workflow to have your network documentation reviewed, risks remediated, and residual risk/security controls accepted. For Federal Government entities, it's in this step where their organization's enterprise network's "risk baseline" is approved. Additionally, networks are authorized for production within specific time frames (i.e., until future revalidation). In the private/commercial world, there is no formal process like NIST RMF for the "authorization" of networks. However, this is a method I use to implement an abbreviated "Authorize" process for the networks under my pervue by focusing on the establishment of my company's enterprise "risk baseline" and then continually testing and validating the selected security controls. Even as a security manager for an SMB, you can do an abbreviated version of this process to understand your company's risks and orchestrate a response to manage it.

In "Authorize," security managers should begin the process by first reviewing the resources and timelines of all active security projects. Next, keep in mind which of these projects are considered critical by the security team because they are correcting identified security "opportunities" or implementing new controls for future organizational plans. As stated, in this step, continually try to validate the risk baseline that was previously established during the assessment of the company's networks, applications, and business processes. For me, the focus on continually testing and validating is because I seek to confirm my current risk exposure baseline and verify the maturity assumptions of deployed security controls.

One major issue I find during this process is that it's tough to produce accurate monetary values for my organization's risk exposure. I have found that I can review the technology portfolio of my organization and assemble a risk matrix based on the installed hardware and software solutions. I can also develop a risk maturity score using industry standards like the Center for Internet Security's Critical Security Controls framework (CIS Controls, 2019). However, even with these methodologies, I still can't adequately answer questions like:

- "How much would a security breach cost us?"

- "Do we have enough cyber insurance to cover our risk exposure?"

- "You want these funds to help us be more secure, how much risk in $$$ are you reducing if your project is funded?"

As the security manager for an SMB, you will be asked similar questions, and they are just as critical. If you knew the cost of an average data breach or the amount of risk you were reducing due to current security projects, you could strategically prioritize the design and management of the business's security program. My last point for this step is that in "Authorize," you will discover that your organization's risk exposure is not static. In fact, it is very dynamic, and it will change over time as new technologies are added to the company's business portfolio. Due to this constant change, do not be afraid to challenge your assumptions. Test the maturity of your security program controls continuously and corroborate your risk baseline because, through this process of managing risk, you will provide strategic business value to your company.

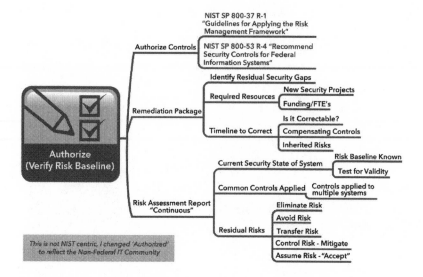

Authorize (Verify Risk Baseline)

6. Continually Monitor (Security Controls)

As with "Assessment," this last step in the enterprise risk management lifecycle is **also present in the cybersecurity lifecycle. In this final step of both lifecycles, we note there are five main components:**

● Monitor Controls

● Incident/Security Breach

● Log Collection/Analysis

● Third Party (Threat Intelligence Feeds)

● **Risk Monitoring**

For the sake of brevity, since our discussion is on risk management and its lifecycle, we will only talk about the final component, "**Risk Monitoring.**" I cover the first four components in my first series of articles on cybersecurity as a lifecycle; these articles are *Cybersecurity, the Continuous Lifecycle Part 1 & 2*[36].

Risk Monitoring ‑ This unique component is centered on tracking the organization's identified risks, monitoring residual risks (what is left after remediation), and identifying new threats to the business. The purpose of risk monitoring is to determine if the controls put in place to reduce risk are effective. Security managers will not only need to monitor current controls; they will also need to monitor the company's risk exposure due to on-going projects and continually verify that documented risk assumptions are correct. Risk monitoring consists of five techniques:

- Risk Response Audits

  Examine the effectiveness of an organization's response to remediating risk. Typically examines the organization's responses to avoiding, transferring, or mitigating specific risk exposures.

- Risk Process Reviews

  Examine risk throughout the lifecycle of a system, workflow, or process. If the identified risks change the selected risk, the management team will submit recommendations for remediation to the company's executive leadership team.

- Risk Value Analysis

  Assessing risk impact through:

  o Qualitative Analysis

    Assess the impact and likelihood of identified risk. Prioritize the risk based on impact to business operations. Security or risk managers will evaluate the probability

---

[36] *Cyber-Security, the Continuous Life-Cycle (Part I & II)*, Hayslip, Gary 2016, First published on *LinkedIn Pulse*.

and consequences, measuring the results with the high, moderate, or low rating.

○   <u>Quantitative Analysis</u>

Analyze the probability of each numerically identified risk and its consequences on business operations. Security or risk managers will use tools such as interviewing, sensitivity analysis, decision tree analysis, or simulations to provide data on the potential impact on the business.

● <u>Risk Performance Measurement</u>

Security or risk managers compare accomplishments during operations to track for trends and reduce risk exposure to the organization.

● <u>Risk Response Planning</u>

Security or risk managers employ monitoring techniques to detect and respond to risk-involved incidents. Develop options for the business with actions assigned to specific teams/individuals to respond to a particular risk event.

○   Ensure that risks are properly addressed with responses that mitigate the identified risk.

o   Responses should reflect the severity of the risk, be cost-effective, and be within the time frame necessary to have a positive impact. The time frame will be based on business requirements. I have seen critical operations require response times in minutes versus hours or days.

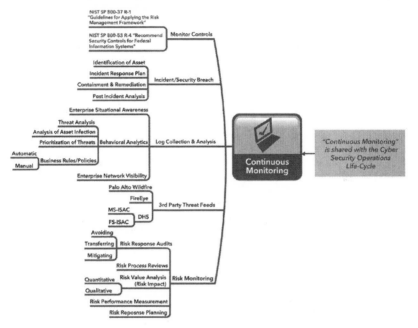

Continuous Monitoring

As we complete risk monitoring, please note that the methodologies used here to monitor and verify an organization's risk can be used by the security team to plan for the proper response procedures. These procedures can lead to the reassessment of controls, new projects to remediate previously unknown issues, or the decommissioning of security controls that are no longer required. Having the proper documentation, procedures, and frameworks in place is critical in this final step to ensure the risk/security picture being monitored by the security program is an accurate baseline for your organization. Now I understand that these risk response procedures may not be within your SMB's level of experience, and that is all right. Reach out to a trusted partner and have them assist you. With their help, you should be able to manage risk remediation/monitoring operations.

This risk management lifecycle and the ecosystem it creates is how I train my teams to view enterprise risk management and cybersecurity as inter-linked continuous strategic processes. In writing this chapter, I wanted to provide the security professional leading security efforts at an SMB a picture of how each step in the lifecycle and ecosystem is interconnected and impacts the next. Finally, I sincerely hope you have found the knowledge in this chapter to be of value.

Chapter 17

An MSP's View on SMB Risk

In Chapter 18, I discuss the considerations SMBs and their security managers should consider when they select a managed service provider (MSP) or a managed security services provider (MSSP) for external technology and security services. However, I would first like you to consider another view, and that is the view of the MSP itself. It is this perspective that I find interesting because each potential SMB client is unique, with technology, processes, compliance, and data requirements that can range from easy-to-manage to extensive and complex.

This chapter will be a discussion between myself and an MSP about various SMB risks and how they might manage them. I want this chapter to provide SMBs and their security managers with a window into how they may be evaluated for critical services when working with potential MSP partners. I am providing this resource to you, security manager, not only to help you understand how your company is evaluated, but to help you in your professional growth as a security executive. It is good to have multiple viewpoints on business risk. With this information you can help your company negotiate a compromise when there are issues with an MSP vendor, and as the senior security leader you will be dealing with issues.

As we begin, I want to state I am not currently nor have I ever managed an MSP; however, in my previous roles I have worked with and advised many of them. It's that experience, plus my 20 years in technology and security, evaluating the risk exposure of my organization and their strategic business operations, that provide the insight for this chapter. Please note as we begin the issues that follow are not all-inclusive. They are just some issues I have seen MSPs review when selecting new clients based on the client's current technologies, the industries they compete in, and finally, their ongoing business practices. For each issue, I shall discuss what concerns me, and hopefully that dialogue can assist actual MSPs in making better-informed decisions, and SMBs in maturing their business practices.

Some potential risks I believe an MSP would screen for are as follows:

1. Does the prospective SMB client understand their industry's compliance/regulation requirements?

I bring this up because I have found numerous times that SMBs hyper-focused on revenue miss new regulations that might significantly impact them. When looking at a new client, I would be concerned if the company and its security manager didn't have a healthy respect for any compliance regime that applied to their industry. They should also be able to speak to how they are currently managing those requirements. I would also want to know if the SMB had any compliance certifications and review previous audit or inspection documents to verify how well the security manager was maintaining them. This issue is primarily a discussion on the risk that an MSP may be liable for if they provide IT/security services to an SMB in a regulated industry such as healthcare, where they may be classified as a business associate of a covered entity, or the financial sector.

2. Does the prospective client have an accurate list of what technologies/applications they use for business?

This question is one of the critical building blocks for a mature cyber-hygiene process. It involves SMBs keeping track of the technologies they are using. One of the core issues that would concern me as an MSP is whether they have a current inventory process in place and do they have current licensing for all applications they currently have in production? Many companies think they know which applications are in use. Still, employees have a habit of using technologies they are comfortable with and over time the company's technology inventory gets out of date. An MSP, who will be onboarding a client like this, will want to know if this inventory information is up to date so they can delineate what they will support and what the customer will manage. I have found, as a security and risk practitioner, you can't protect it if you don't know it's there.

3. Does the prospective client have an accurate list of vendors and partners they share information with or allow to access their networks?

The risk equation here that concerns me as an MSP is another cybersecurity factor that weighs heavily on today's security managers, which is one of visibility. I would think most potential clients would know who they are doing business with and who has access to their networks for maintenance and support. I believe an MSP would want to know about these agreements, primarily if they were providing network management services. My concern here as an MSP is one of risk exposure if there is a breach due to one of these vendors. Where does that liability fall, and how will the incident be managed?

4. Is the prospective client using BYOD?

In today's fast-moving business environment, I think almost every organization is using some form of BYOD technology or remote access application for its employees. My concern, from a security standpoint, is how the customer is currently managing its BYOD environment. When looking at a prospective customer with employees using their own devices to conduct business, an MSP must think about how to handle the risk created by the non-company devices. Is there a technology already in place that makes sure employees' devices have the latest anti-virus and software patches? Is there a technology that tracks employees who have remote access to

SMB-owned networks? Does the SMB have business processes in place defining how these accounts, devices, and data are accessed and used by these disparate technologies? These questions are critical in understanding this risk because an MSP will want to know what their responsibilities are. A hybrid BYOD environment can be very challenging to manage and protect.

5. Is the prospective client using a process for employee onboarding/off-boarding?

Some SMBs outsource this to a third party. The concern I have here is if I am an MSP that will be providing help desk services and account management services, I would want to know if they have processes in place for how they manage the lifecycle of employees' access and accounts. Do they have procedures to remove data access and disable user accounts when the employee leaves the organization? Are there procedures for provisioning user accounts with appropriate levels of access for new employees? Are user accounts and their access levels regularly audited to verify that access is still appropriate? The answers to these questions will provide an MSP with insight into how mature the SMB is and whether the MSP will need to remediate or create an identity and access management program for the SMB.

6. Does the prospective client have on-site IT/security staff, and what is their responsibility?

For those SMBs that do not want to outsource their IT and security operations to an MSP entirely, the answer to this question can be revealing in terms of how they want to manage their risk. The reason I say this is because what I typically see is that small SMBs have IT and security services entirely outsourced so they can focus on revenue and growth. However, as the SMB matures and operations grow in complexity, there tends to be a move to bring some critical activities back in-house, believing it is better to manage risk than continue expanding services. The data collected from the above question will provide an understanding of where the organization is within this cycle of growth and will also offer insight into how they plan to manage their liabilities. As an MSP, my concerns about this issue are two-fold. First, I would be concerned if there are specific business operations that are deemed critical, with significant risk exposure, that the MSP is being asked to manage. This problem typically happens when SMBs don't have staff with the expertise to remediate issues, and a decision is made to transfer these risks to an MSP to oversee. The second concern I have is how any IT/security staff already employed by the SMB will operate with the MSP's teams. Both of these issues will require the MSP to decide if they have the technology, personnel, and experience to handle this risk exposure, and whether they can work with on-site staff in a partner relationship. If there are any doubts concerning this, then they may wish to document liability constraints in their SLAs or decline to provide service to the SMB because the risk to the MSP's operations could be too high to manage efficiently.

7. Is the prospective client planning to expand or implement new technologies?

The growth issue is of concern if the SMB is on track to grow in size and will require a breadth of services beyond what the MSP currently provides. Expansion may sound like it would be a good thing because an MSP could earn more revenue. However, if the MSP doesn't have infrastructure that can scale or enough personnel to meet its contractual commitments, this scenario could quickly become a nightmare. Regarding new technologies, the concern is about the MSP providing quality service. New technologies can put a support strain on the MSP. The MSP could also be placed in a situation by the SMB to support a third-party contractor who is managing this new technology. Both situations could result in significant risk to the MSP by impacting its ability to provide quality services to its other customers.

8. How is the prospective client managing its data?

This issue has the most risk and impact on an organization. It is a strategic discussion on whether the potential customer understands what types of data it has and what types are required to be successful as a business. They should also be able to answer questions about who has access to their sensitive data and how this sensitive data is being protected, stored, and destroyed when no longer required. My concern when getting answers to these questions is making sure the customer is doing some form of data governance. If an MSP is being hired to manage an SMB's data assets and its infrastructure, then they will want to know what technologies the SMB is currently using to control its information. The MSP should verify that the SMB has documented where its data is stored, the current location of its sensitive business data, if this critical information is encrypted, and, finally, the location of those encryption keys. One last significant concern that I would have about how an SMB manages its data is focused on the processes they have for backing up sensitive data. Is the SMB using a data backup process? The MSP will need to understand what technology its potential customer is using for backups and when the backups were last tested.

9. Is the prospective client following any current industry best practices, industry compliance regimes, or industry risk management frameworks?

This issue falls in parallel with the first question I proposed as a risk that the MSP would need to verify. The concern is whether the MSP has the ability to maintain the security control requirements mandated for HIPAA or PCI DSS compliance, or to implement a NIST or ISO 27001 framework or standard. Some MSPs will have the expertise and experienced staff who understand these security controls and have the technologies in place to maintain them. If not, then this becomes an issue the MSP itself may have to outsource to a third party if it wants to manage the regulated SMB's requirements efficiently. My concern is that the skillsets required for this can be expensive, and if not done correctly, can expose the MSP to significant liability risk. This should be evaluated when reviewing whether to onboard an SMB client who operates in a regulated industry space or requires industry certifications.

10. Does the prospective client have any current enterprise IT or cybersecurity programs?

This final concern is one about integration if an SMB client has current operational IT or security programs. How will the MSP fit into the ongoing business operations and not impact the SMB? Integrating with an existing program can impinge on an MSP's ability to provide contracted services. The MSP may be required to support an IT or security program that has more stringent security controls than the industry standard. These demanding requirements have the potential to expose an MSP to not meeting specific levels of service. Also, in meeting the unique service requirements, the MSP may incur undocumented costs that could impede its ability to serve its other customers. This is a challenging issue. The MSP would generally want customers to have some level of risk governance. However, if meeting the security controls required creates a significant burden on an MSP's operations, then the MSP must reevaluate whether they want the potential client's business.

Risk, whether viewed from the SMB or MSP point of view, is relatively similar, with the difference being a matter of scale and complexity. One organization looks to acquire services, and the other seeks to provide them. Both want to conduct these operations with the least amount of disruption to current business activities and at minimal cost to their respective organizations. The differences I find are that to the SMB, the services they require are a commodity that has unique requirements and risk exposure that can be limited and defined with specific security controls and contractual agreements. For the MSP, however, it's a different story because the commodity it provides with a particular level of risk for one SMB can create an entirely different level of risk for another SMB. Now factor in that MSPs can have a large number of SMB customers, each of them with varying levels of risk, and the result is a portfolio that can be quite extensive and limit an MSP's ability to be innovative and grow as a company. I see this liability as an opportunity for an MSP. It is why I believe MSPs need to periodically assess their customers' risks to establish their exposure baseline. Then, with this understanding of the hazards they face, a more informed decision on what risk they are willing to accept or manage can be be made for the betterment of their business and the services they provide to all of their SMB clients.

As I close this chapter, I hope it has provided you with some insight into risks that will need to be reviewed when you, in your capacity as a security manager for an SMB, seek to contract services out to an MSP/MSSP. This is not everything that will need to be analyzed by an MSP as they discuss with you what security services you require. Hopefully, having read this chapter, you will be better prepared for these discussions as you help your business select the level of service it requires – good luck!

Chapter 18

Questions SMBs Should Ask Potential Managed Service Providers

It can be daunting for an SMB to step into the often-unfamiliar world of cybersecurity, where they can at times be inundated with technical terms (and where they can face real consequences for making an incorrect decision). This is why I advocate for an SMB to employ a security manager once they are mature enough to support a security executive and formal security program. However, not all SMBs are at that level. Employing an MSP or MSSP is often in the best interest of SMBs who require security services but may not have the expertise to select and manage all of the critical resources they require.

In the Ponemon Institute study on the state of cybersecurity for SMBs[37], they researched and documented statistics on which threats to their operations SMBs are experiencing and the impact of these incidents on their growing businesses. I found several findings to be startling, including:

- Only 14% of those surveyed felt their companies could mitigate their cyber risks.

- 55% of those surveyed reported their companies had experienced a cyber-attack in the previous 12 months.

- Finally, those companies that had experienced an incident reported:

---

[37] See the reading list for Section 1

☐ Spending an average of $879,582 as a result of the damage or theft to IT assets.

☐ The cost of disruptions to normal business operations was on average $955,429.

I believe these numbers are only scratching the surface of what the SMB community is experiencing as they connect their businesses to the world's digital infrastructure. Many of these organizations are focusing scarce resources on growing their operations and outsourcing the management of their IT and security services to third parties. 34% of those surveyed reported using a managed service provider (MSP) or managed security service provider (MSSP) due to a lack of personnel, budget, or experience with security technologies. An MSP/MSSP can, in effect, become the IT department or security team the growing SMB needs, allowing the SMB to focus its resources on maturing and growing its business operations.

One-third of the surveyed SMBs are already using trusted third parties to manage their IT and security services. Here I want to focus on what concerns the undecided SMBs and their security/IT managers should consider if they wish to select an MSP/MSSP partner. The following factors, I believe, are areas of interest that an SMB's leadership team should review when choosing a strategic partner they can trust.

1. Financial stability, in it for the long haul

An MSP/MSSP's length of time in the industry doesn't mean they are trustworthy, nor does it say they are financially stable. Many of them are SMBs themselves, so I would recommend that the security and IT managers research the provider's annual reports or financial statements if available. Don't be afraid to ask for proof that they are financially stable. You are going to trust them to support your company, and you want to make sure they are there when you need them.

2. Solid reputation for customer service

It's important to make sure that the MSP/MSSP hired to support the business has a solid reputation for providing professional service with a track record of exceptional customer care. I would recommend the MSP/MSSP provide customer references and testimonials for the security manager and IT manager to review and be sure to spend the time to reach out and speak to these references.

3. Industry knowledge, be a partner

The MSP/MSSP should be knowledgeable about your SMB's industry and able to make recommendations for possible improved work processes, industry training, and software solutions. An MSP/MSSP that operates in your industry should understand the challenges your business faces and the compliance requirements or regulations that may apply to current operations, and they should have an understanding of where they can provide efficiencies. In speaking with the MSP/MSSP, use this as an opportunity to verify their experience, and look for industry-related certifications. If possible, talk with several of the MSP/MSSP's employees who have experience in your industry, visit the MSP/MSSP after hours to validate whether they do, indeed, operate effectively 24 x 7. This information will enable you to make a more informed decision on whether they can meet your requirements and whether they possess the level of expertise required for your business operations.

4. Menus of services, they are here to help

The needs of SMBs can be quite diverse. MSPs and MSSPs should be able to provide a list of technology-based services such as the management of and updates to business software, deployment of security patches, antivirus and firewall protection, and risk assessment and vulnerability remediation. There are also non-technology related services that can be purchased, such as a block of hours for certified professionals to provide niche services for the SMB. This can be helpful if the company already has an IT or security team but needs extra assistance for unique projects or strategic business initiatives. As the security manager for your SMB, make sure you understand the services a prospective partner has to offer you and whether these delivered services have additional costs or are included as part of an overall per seat price.

5. Are 24 x 7 service and remote monitoring available?

A mature MSP/MSSP will have invested in dedicated continuous monitoring technologies that can help them identify issues before they significantly impact your business networks. You should choose a provider that has a well-developed service team that excels at system monitoring for technologies such as workstations, servers, network devices, firewalls, routers, and switches, regardless of their deployed locations. They should be available to provide service regardless of the day, time, or holiday, 24 hours a day, 365 days a year. Your business and its IT/security assets don't rest, so you need a dedicated partner that is available to you. Just understand that this level of service costs more and the MSP/MSSP should be able to provide information on these costs clearly and concisely.

6. What types of support does the MSP/MSSP offer?

An MSP/MSSP should provide more than one kind of support service due to SMBs having diverse technology requirements. Some MSP/MSSPs provide remote support, which can help resolve minor issues quickly. However, onsite support by selected IT/security professionals can genuinely help your SMB be more efficient and reduce the impact of an issue on business operations. When choosing an MSP/MSSP, you will want to understand if the selected provider can accommodate regularly scheduled preventive maintenance for assets like servers and workstations – and you will want to verify they can be hands-on when necessary. Again, don't forget that some of these services may have additional costs. As the security manager, make sure you understand these costs because I am sure you will be operating on a limited budget and you don't want to be surprised.

7. Should have demonstrated skills and experience

Any MSP/MSSP being reviewed as a possible partner should, at a minimum, employ personnel who have proven skill sets that go beyond basic software installation, maintenance, and upgrades. SMBs will likely need some advanced IT/security services, such as database management, virtualization, cloud deployment, security monitoring, and cross-platform integration. A mature provider should have demonstrated expertise in these technology models to meet your growing strategic business requirements, or partnerships where they can pass through a required service when needed.

8. MSP/MSSP should ask you questions; it's all about risk

A provider should ask your small business questions as well. They should want to know information like do you require unique resources for meeting compliance or industry regulations? They should want to understand how your current business networks are built, what types of data your stakeholders need, and how this data should be accessed, stored, backed up, and decommissioned. They should ask questions about how your information is transported and if it stays on-premise, or does it reside in public/private cloud instances? The reason for these questions is an MSP/MSSP will be accepting risk when they agree to provide services to your company. Because of this risk exposure, they should be asking you questions so they can better understand how to support your business without endangering themselves with unnecessary risks.

9. Global services, are they available?

Besides providing services for your small business' current business sites, what if you have sites, networks, systems, etc. in multiple countries? This may not be a current requirement. However, if the SMB were to expand globally, are the existing contracted IT/security services the SMB depends on available with local language support for foreign subsidiaries in these new locations? If not, this isn't a deal breaker. However, you should check and see that if your MSP/MSSP is not able to provide these services, they at least have partners that you can leverage to access these services for your growing company.

10. Cybersecurity hygiene, can you at least get the basics?

One last recommendation – does the selected provider understand cybersecurity hygiene and does their menu of services align with these necessary controls for enterprise risk management? Not all MSP/MSSPs can provide every service an SMB requires; with that said, not all SMBs can afford to purchase those same services either. In selecting a service provider you, as the security manager, should at least make sure they meet some basic security controls. These should include at least asset inventory, patch management, access management, continuous monitoring, vulnerability scanning, AV, and firewall management. There are numerous services that I could list, but as a growing small business, you need to ensure they can consistently provide you with the basics to protect your organization and you should ensure that your master services agreement (MSA) has breach notification language.

The recommendations above are not all-inclusive; many others may apply to an SMB depending on its industry. It is essential that before an SMB and its IT/security managers begin to seek a service partner, they should thoroughly understand the current IT and security environments, including regulatory and compliance needs. They should then find partners that help them be more efficient in reducing risk exposure to the business. I currently see the SMB community expanding exponentially. It is a dynamic community willing to be the first to leverage new technologies. However, it is also a community that is heavily targeted by cybercriminals. Because of tight resources, many of these businesses may lack the security resources they need to prevent a cyber intrusion that could have devastating consequences for their company and its customers. These consequences are why I added this chapter to the book. I hope these evaluation factors provide some insight for security managers as they help their SMB make educated decisions on what services are required.

I'll leave you with one final note. As a security leader, you are not going to know everything; it's OK to ask for help; it's OK to collaborate with peers and admit you need their viewpoint on an issue. It's not OK to ignore your risk. Today all entities in our connected world are targeted – good luck protecting yours.

Reading List for Section 5

1. *COBIT 5*, ISACA 2019 https://cobitonline.isaca.org/about
2. *PCI Data Security Standard,* PCI Council, 2018
   https://www.pcisecuritystandards.org/document_library
3. *Health Information Protection and Accountability Act,* Department of
   Health and Human Services (HHS), 2019
   https://www.hhs.gov/hipaa/index.html
4. *Service Organization Controls Type 2* (SOC-2™) for Service
   Organizations, AICPA 2019
   https://www.aicpa.org/interestareas/frc/assuranceadvisoryservices
   /aicpasoc2report.html
5. *CIS Controls*, Center for Internet Security, 2019
   https://www.cisecurity.org/controls/
6. *Security & Privacy Controls*, NIST Computer Science Resource
   Center, 2015
   https://csrc.nist.gov/publications/detail/sp/800-53/rev-4/final

Building and Executing Your Plan

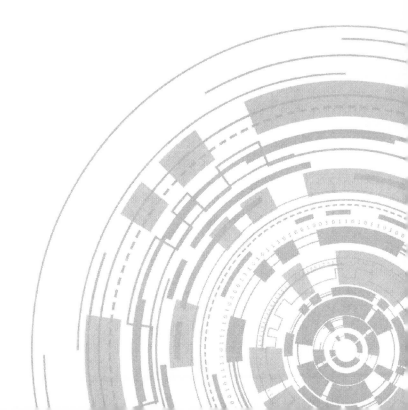

With all the elements in place, it is time to create your strategic plan and step up to full execution.

To help with this last phase, Chapter 19 provides a list of fundamentals for your plan. Then Chapter 20 helps you build the plan itself. Chapter 21 helps you identify the keys to your success as an executive in the company.

Finally, Chapter 22 provides the views for the CEO. If your CEO has questions about your role or your program, this is an excellent resource. If you want to know how to best educate your CEO, have them start by reading this chapter.

After the conclusion, you will find a glossary of terms and a collection of resources you should find helpful.

Chapter 19

A Security Manager's Seven Fundamentals

Several years ago, I received an early-morning phone call at home from a member of my security staff. Our security operations center had just contacted us, reporting anomalous data traffic. They believed we had several assets that were infected with malware. As I listened to the incident response team triage the event, I thought to myself, "What can I do as a security executive to better protect my organization?"

At that time in my role, I had numerous networks and legacy assets under my purview, and even though I had a solid security program, I didn't feel we were doing enough to address our risk. What fundamentals could I incorporate? To answer this question, I started to review and document how I would continuously analyze and upgrade my security systems and deployed security controls. I eventually settled on seven steps I call my Seven Fundamentals. These are the processes I use as a CISO to view my security program, understand its dependencies, and continuously review for improvement. They have become one of several templates I use to measure the maturity of my security stack and my overall security program. These fundamentals should provide you with a set of tools to use in protecting your business and its critical assets.

Here are the first four of my Security Manager Fundamentals

Enumerate. As a security leader, I find it crucial that I understand what is on my company's networks, where the devices are located, and what applications and data they require. Enumeration provides that information – and it's fundamental to cyber hygiene.

Part of the enumeration process is the discovery of hosts and devices on a network, typically using standard industry tools that incorporate discovery protocols such as ICMP and SNMP. Once scans are complete this data is collected and organized to document well-known services and operating systems. This data can then be used by the security teams to provide insight into the architecture of corporate networks and to update the current configuration management database (CMDB). This foundational step feeds not just my cybersecurity and risk management programs, but it is also required for IT, change management, governance, risk and compliance. Without an accurate inventory, it is extremely hard to manage risk and protect the company's digital assets.

Consolidate. With an updated inventory, you, as the security manager, can now identify what could be consolidated. For example, can your SMB reduce its servers and server locations to more efficiently use space and resources? Can servers be virtualized or upgraded to new hardware to occupy less rack space and consume less power?

I look at consolidation as another foundational control. While keeping business needs in mind, I review my security portfolio's hardware and software tools continuously to see if there is anything I can consolidate or decommission. If I can reduce my costs and consolidate the assets my team must manage without impacting the services we provide to the business, I believe it's required of me as a security leader to investigate that possibility.

Mitigate. For this step, I review the potential impact of identified risks on the organization's business operations. This process is continuous. As we add new technologies to the company's portfolio or change deployed applications, we need to reassess security risks. If risks are identified, then we employ appropriate and cost-effective controls to mitigate the risk to an acceptable level.

The security manager and their team need to manage this process continuously and report the results to their company's executive staff periodically. I recommend that security managers collaborate with business stakeholders and use current company business objectives as guidelines to prioritize any identified risks that must be mitigated.

Integrate. I don't want my organization's security platform to resemble a do-it-yourself dashboard representing multiple islands of isolated technology held together by virtual duct tape. Security teams need to assess the integration of security components continually. Where appropriate, integration provides operating efficiencies and more visibility into deployed security assets, networks, and risks. As a security manager, you should always review your security stack to see where you can integrate your selected technologies for efficiency and automate routine tasks.

I would rather have my selected solutions connected via technology, such as through APIs, providing me with an overall view of risk in one platform. I know many organizations have critical legacy systems, and no one wants to touch them because they work. I understand as I have been in that situation multiple times. However, every time I have upgraded and integrated my security stack, its new capabilities and efficiencies have paid dividends.

I am aware that integrating security systems is not an easy process. Security vendors often force organizations to purchase all the platform's components to get full functionality. Or they provide minimal customer service, instead opting to charge for assistance in the form of professional services. But if you can make a business case for integration, it will often result in reduced labor required to triage an incident or in greater visibility to strategic threats facing the organization.

How I advance my security programs into innovation

Over the past ten years, I have watched the security manager and CISO roles evolve into strategic partnerships with the business when executive leadership champions them. I have also witnessed a changing environment that seems to open more doorways to attackers than security professionals can close – from new malware types to previously unknown vulnerabilities at the supply chain and hardware level.

It was this drive to perform as a valued business partner that pushed me to consider new approaches to managing my organization's risk, which resulted in these seven fundamentals. In crafting my Security Manager Fundamentals, I learned to accept the fact that security and risk management programs are not made to be static but instead need to be flexible so they can adjust to new threats, new technologies, and resource constraints. As security leaders, we must be innovative and willing to make changes to our security program and its services so they are focused on providing the correct type of cybersecurity and risk management services to the business. The final three fundamentals are advanced concepts that even an SMB can employ when they approach them correctly.

Here are the final three of my seven Security Manager Fundamentals

Innovate. As technology advances, cybercriminals are continually innovating and deploying new capabilities, thereby increasing the threats companies face. Security leaders, in turn, need to be comfortable with this evolution and be flexible in looking at new defensive security technologies.

The cyber hygiene basics – configuration management, access control, network segmentation, patch management, and network monitoring – can remove most of the cyber risk facing an SMB and allow its security manager and team to identify new technologies and services that provide value to the business.

There are risks associated with being innovative. This is exactly why I believe it is imperative to have the security basics done first. With cyber hygiene baked into the security program like muscle memory, the security manager then gains the freedom to try new technologies and processes, becoming more efficient with the resources they have, while still managing risk.

Automate. The days of having a security analyst review logs manually and then manually investigate an anomalous finding are over. As cybercriminals use automation to deploy new threats quickly, security leaders must look at automation to improve the capabilities of their security assets, risk management controls, and security teams. That's the only way to defend against today's fast-moving threats.

As a CISO, I regularly review my security program's technologies to identify where I can automate data (or labor) intensive services such as threat-intelligence analysis, security rules enforcement, and the review of logs for anomalous behavior. I believe automated analysis allows for more effective use of resources, and as a security manager for an SMB, I don't believe you can ignore an efficiency like the power of automation.

Orchestrate. Orchestrating is about connecting security tools and integrating different types of security systems. In today's technology environments, the sheer volume of data and logs generated can be massive, and this flood of data can quickly lead to alert fatigue and human error. With security orchestration, a security team can coordinate the flow of data and tasks (e.g., monitoring IPS alerts) by integrating existing tools and processes into repeatable workflows.

I look at security orchestration as a security platform to connect my various assets, tools, and processes. This allows my team to leverage automation efficiently. Using orchestration, security leaders gain more value from their limited resources and replace slow, linear processes with fast, contextual decision making.

I believe orchestration is a security-program necessity because of the complexity of current security platforms and the propensity for human error. But I have found orchestration requires that I complete the other fundamentals first.

I have found that the Seven Fundamentals lead to a stable security program, and I hope they help you as you build your security program and lead your team. If you implement these fundamentals as part of your security effort, they become the building blocks of your cybersecurity program. Then you only need to monitor them continuously, tune them, test them, and use them to make security operations more manageable and effective. Remember, even as a security manager for an SMB you are not too small to use these steps to be more effective and grow as a security leader. Good luck!

Chapter 20

Building Your Cybersecurity Strategic Plan

Technology changes at a rate most businesses can't keep pace with, and this lag introduces considerable risk to a company's business operations. To manage this risk, many security leaders must wade into an ever-changing, turbulent network landscape and seek to establish some order through their selected security frameworks and controls. These security leaders also apply best-practice approaches to this diverse risk portfolio using traditional concepts such as zero-trust and layered security technologies and services.

I believe this approach needs to change, especially for SMBs. This approach was created for centralized, managed networks that many of us in security first started our careers with years ago. Today's networks typically don't have fully defined perimeters. They are designed for the mobile worker and geo-dispersed teams with numerous third-party connections to vendors and trusted partners. It's these new network infrastructures that exist in the cloud, in shared data centers, and on mobile devices that force SMBs and their security managers to reevaluate plans for how to implement and manage the business's cybersecurity program without impeding new business opportunities.

Strategic plans, in essence, are cybersecurity roadmaps that establish the pathways a security manager will follow to mature their risk management approach while protecting their company. These plans should describe how the security program will preserve and share information, counter new and evolving threats, and support the integration of cybersecurity as a best practice for everyday business operations. A strategic plan should note the *"current state"* of security practices and describe near-term objectives to be addressed in the next 12 months, midterm goals in the next 18-24 months, and long-term objectives over the next 36 months. The security manager and critical stakeholders usually develop this plan and it should be considered a living document. The vision, goals, and objectives of this plan should be reviewed at least annually by the security manager and the SMB's executive leadership team, with changes incorporated and new initiatives scheduled accordingly.

To begin, security managers must understand the current security state of their SMB. This effort will require an inventory and continuous scanning of assets such as hardware, software, network configurations, policies, security controls, prior audit findings, etc.

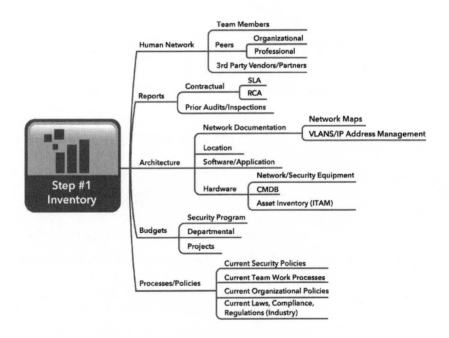

Step #1 Inventory

The goal is to gather information on the current technology and application portfolios and current business plans, and then gain an understanding of the critical data types required by business stakeholders. As this data is assessed, security managers should then meet with business unit stakeholders to establish the value of this collected information. It is critical to have business unit leaders assist in this endeavor. They can provide an accurate understanding of the value of each asset (data, system, or application) based on the time, effort, and resources it would take to replace it if it became unavailable due to a cyber incident. A quick point I want to make here is that these steps are the same ones that you, as a security manager, have taken to establish your security program and implement some resiliency initiatives for your SMB. Remember, cybersecurity is a lifecycle, many of its practices have multiple uses, and as you mature in your role, you will find ways to tailor these processes to fit your needs while still managing risk for the business.

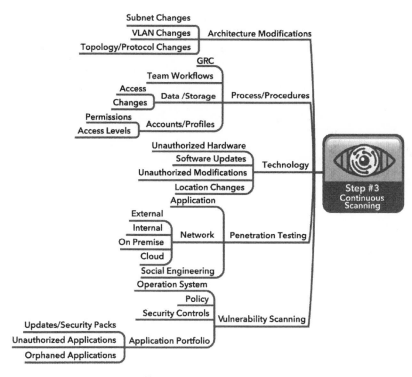

Step #3 Continuous Scanning

The security manager now has a current view of resources and their prioritized value to the business. We also know the requirements for the company to operate and the financial impact on operations should a security incident render an asset or business process unavailable. The next step is to take this information and develop a more refined look at the business's security and risk requirements. Here security managers use a familiar approach: select a risk framework (ISO, NIST, COBIT) and conduct a risk assessment. The result of the assessment is used to establish or update a current risk exposure baseline for the SMB.

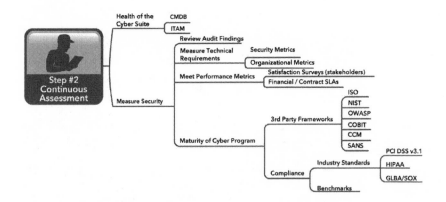

Step #2 Continuous Assessment

In planning an assessment, security managers begin by using a risk management framework as the template to assess all collected security information. Once the evaluation has been completed, it is reviewed, and any new areas of potential risk exposure to ongoing business activities are identified, documented, and prioritized. With this new insight, the security manager and their team can now begin to develop their program's strategic plan. The steps above were essential for the security manager and the SMB because they provide a contextual view of where the organization stands at present with regards to its security practices and what future changes may be required to assist the company in meeting its business objectives. This living document, the strategic plan, will be used by the security manager to guide their organization from its current security state to a future security state where assessed security gaps are addressed, and new services are deployed. The plan should be concise and easy to understand. The security manager and the company's executive leadership team need to be realistic with regard to available resources and allocate funding to those areas of highest risk that are most closely aligned with organizational strategy and priorities.

The components of a cybersecurity strategic plan that I would recommend for an SMB and their security team are as follows:

1. Mission Statement

This is the declaration of the organization's core purpose; it generally doesn't change over time.

> Example of what I have used before: "Develop and execute a proactive, company-wide security program based on the company's strategic business objectives."

2. Vision Statement

This statement is an aspirational description of what an organization would like to achieve.

> Example of what I have seen used: "Incorporate a continuous security mindset into all aspects of our business functions."

3. Introduction

This is a statement about the business and the environment in which the security program currently operates. I have seen the executive leadership team use this section to state their support of the security program and why it is critical for the business.

4. Governance

This part of the strategic plan is where the security manager explains how it will be managed, who will audit the program's processes, and how changes will be implemented over time. Remember, this is a long-term plan, so ensure that you have these procedures documented. You may also want to reference budgeting, staffing and other required resources.

5. Strategic Objectives

This is the core part of a security program's strategic plan; it will be developed and maintained by the security manager and will contain the objectives identified during the most recent risk assessment that need to be remediated. This section will include the latest assessment results and should have an ongoing project plan listing the various projects that are in the queue; each one should be tracked to a specific security control objective.

Out of this whole document, the strategic objectives are the part that will be continuously updated as projects are completed and the organization is reassessed to establish an updated risk baseline. You may want to transfer this information into a document called a risk register, which can be used by stakeholders to track and review risk over time. In the past I have organized projects and initiatives into a three-year timeline. Understand that you can adjust this three-year schedule depending on the availability of resources or executive sponsorship; plus, the list of projects can be reorganized to meet current business needs or new threats. Each objective will typically have several actions/projects derived from the assessed security function, which need to be completed. An example of a strategic goal is as follows:

- *Security Objective* – Data loss prevention

- **Key Initiative** – Security policy, standards, and guidelines framework *** (These are the actual gaps that were found in the security gap analysis of the current completed risk assessment.

  - ☐ **Enabling Objectives** – Data loss prevention, improved security of system and network services, proactive data management, and governance.

  - ☐ **Description** - Develop, approve, and launch a suite of information security policies, standards, and guidelines based on ISO/IEC27001.

  - ☐ **Key Benefits** - These benefits need to be aligned with the business.

    - Clear security baselines for all departments
    - Policy-based foundation to measure results
    - Consistent application of security controls across the enterprise

  - ☐ **Project** – Listed the technologies, services, etc. that will meet the objective.

The above example is just a basic layout of a strategic goal for a cybersecurity program. Depending on the SMB's maturity, the security manager may list several projects under a specific objective. I have seen security leaders build a strategic plan and then collect all of the projects into a master list. They would then manage that list, and as projects were completed, they would do a new risk baseline assessment. This process is never perfect, but it can be used by security managers to provide executive reports to management that demonstrate the business value a mature cybersecurity program brings to enhancing business operations and enabling new business initiatives.

Chapter 21

Serving as a Security Leader, Five Steps for Success

I have been writing and speaking about the role of the security executive for the last several years. As I have continually acknowledged, the job, whether it's as a security manager or a CISO, is not for the faint of heart. The role at times can be stress-filled, taking a toll on its incumbents that results in medical issues, career burnout, and a continuous shortage of senior security executives. Besides the technical requirements of the job, the role also requires security leaders to work with corporate stakeholders like legal, risk, and compliance teams, interpreting the applicability of numerous federal and state laws, contractual obligations, and compliance regulations. It is these daunting requirements that lead me to include this chapter and discuss with you, an SMB's security manager, another methodology I developed through trial and error to help new security leaders.

I have been in the information technology and cybersecurity fields for over 25 years and have been a CISO for the last fifteen years. It is this experience that helped me develop my five-step approach to improve my organization's cybersecurity strategy and protect its enterprise networks and critical business assets. This process can be used by security professionals taking their first role who need to assess the current health of their security program or by more seasoned professionals who wish to enhance and upgrade a security program they are currently managing. As mentioned, this methodology has five steps, and they are as follows: *Meet & Greet, Inventory, Assessment, Planning, and finally Communicating.*

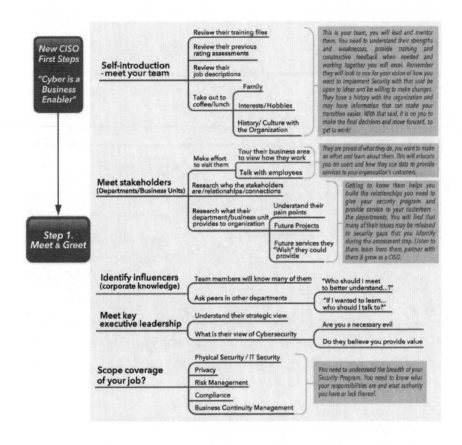

Step 1 Meet & Greet

1. Meet & Greet - "Let's Take a Walk About"

I usually begin this first step by having several in-depth security team meetings and then continue by walking about the organization to meet critical business stakeholders and executive leadership team members. When meeting with the team for the first time, I recommend using this as an opportunity to articulate the security strategy that you, as the security executive for the business, want to implement. Through the resulting dialogue with team members, assess their current skillsets and experience. This assessment and further one-to-one meetings with team members will help you understand if the team currently possesses the skills and expertise to implement your strategy and future projects. If your team lacks experience, you may have to contract a third-party vendor to provide the professional services you require or train team personnel to improve their technical capabilities, or a combination of both.

Next, in meeting with key business stakeholders, I recommend that you be quiet and listen to them talk and be open to their issues. Keep in mind that as the security manager, they are your customers. You provide them with a service, and you need to be mindful that they may have had problems with past security leaders or with how your team has performed. These meetings with stakeholders are a chance for you to hear of any current issues and learn from them which technology, services, data, and personnel are critical for their operations. Use these meetings to establish a relationship and begin to build trust in your team and security program.

Finally, when meeting with executive leadership, just as you did with your stakeholders be quiet and let them talk. In these discussions, you need to visualize how you fit into the overall business culture, how you are going to support current operations, and if you can help manage any key business concerns. Try to help them understand that cybersecurity is a business enabler; it provides a secure foundation for them to innovate and develop new services for the organization. As you finish your walkabout, make sure to spend time with your boss. Whether it's the CIO or another executive, you want to have a good working relationship with them so that you understand the scope of your responsibilities and limitations on your department or budget. It is tough to lead a security team and manage an enterprise cybersecurity program if there is some ambiguity in your role or responsibilities. At the end of the first step, the business knows who you are, and your vision for the security program. Now it's time to educate yourself on the internal components of the business, its technology stack, and your new security portfolio.

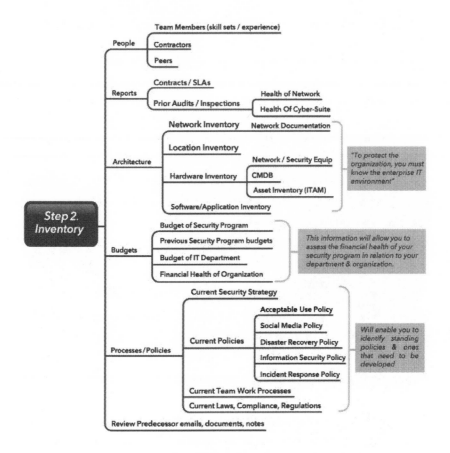

Step 2 Inventory

2. Inventory

When you think of inventories, take an expansive view to include not just assets and software but skills, competencies, vendors, policies, etc. We have discussed inventory numerous times in previous chapters, and all of this attention shows that it's important. As the security manager for your SMB, you will take a more in-depth look at your team and assess their skillsets and experiences. You will look at the contractors that fall under your purview and the services they provide (review contracts and SLA metrics). I have used this exercise to look for trend analysis, so I suggest you look at your current budget and previous security budgets. If you see increases in costs, but little to no increases in new services, that's a red flag. You need to review those anomalies.

If you inherited the security program and want to understand how the business views your security program, it's this budget analysis that will allow you to gain perspective about whether cybersecurity is leveraged to grow the business or seen as a cost center with little value. When you are reviewing your program's budget, I would recommend you also look at your department's budget, and if you have permission, the overall organization's budgets. Putting your budget in context with the rest of the company will help you temper your ask of management.

One of the last things you will do in this step is also one of the most time-consuming. You will need to assess the current network and security architectures, work processes, and standing policies. This part of the process is when you will determine the "cyber hygiene" baseline of your organization. Be forewarned; you will find policies and procedures that will need to be improved upon and possible architectural changes that may need to be implemented to reduce risk exposures to the business. Add these findings to your risk register for future remediation. You will also find that you need to collect and verify that you have up-to-date network documentation such as network maps, subnet and VLAN lists, and asset management documentation.

These documents will provide you with visibility into how your network and security suite is configured and help you identify areas for improvement. I have found from my own experience that many times companies believe they have a solid understanding of their networks and applications. However, when the data is collected and analyzed, the reality can be quite different. Unknown network architectures, data access by unauthorized personnel, remote network connections and extra third-party vendors are typical, and don't be surprised that they have never been adequately documented. When you reach the end of this step, I strongly recommended that you take a break and review your notes on what has been found. With a firm understanding of your environment, review any predecessor's records, emails, and documents.

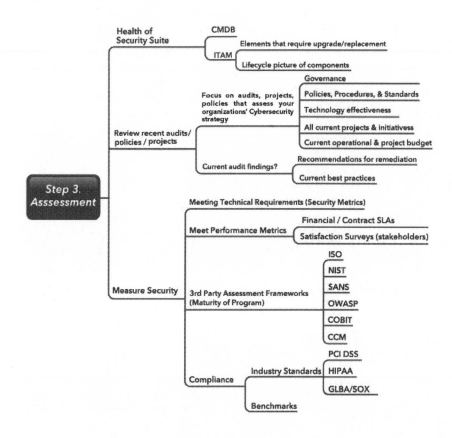

Step 3 Assessment

3. Assessment

In the previous step you gained visibility into the company's technology and security portfolios as you conducted an inventory. Now it's time to get your hands dirty. As the senior security professional, it is critical that you get a better understanding of how the network and cybersecurity stacks are architected, how data flows throughout this architecture, and how employees use corporate data. It's in this step that you must assess the health of the cybersecurity suite. Look at installed technologies such as firewalls, AV solutions, EPP/EDR platforms, IDS/IPS sensors, and security procedures such as vulnerability scanning/remediation, and incident response. The newly upgraded network diagrams and documentation from the previous step will be used here to help build a roadmap for follow-on assessment projects. In this stage, the security manager and security team will assess the effectiveness of the present cybersecurity program and document areas for improvement. From experience, I tend to use the NIST and ISO frameworks as templates for the security controls that will be assessed and verify their applicability to my existing network and security architecture.

In this step security managers should review previous third-party assessments, vulnerability assessments, and penetration tests. The security manager and security team will want to review each report's findings and the recommendations for remediation and verify whether the recommendations were ever implemented. This stage is the most technical of the five; it is not uncommon for the security manager to request third-party vendor assistance to conduct these assessments and provide recommendations for improvement. By the end of the assessment step, you should now have a list of security gaps. These gaps will become input for future projects that should be prioritized based on the risk exposure or business impact to the company. We discuss the process of prioritizing this list and turning it into a strategic plan next.

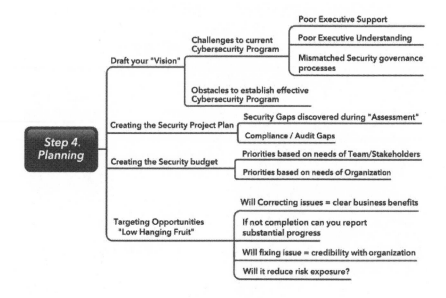

Step 4 Planning

4. Planning

This step can run in parallel with assessment. I have found it to be a continuous process that must be adjusted to the business. The planning step is when the security manager and security team begin to build their program's strategic plan, often called their roadmap. This plan can be brand new, or it can be an enhancement to a current plan, updated to lay out your vision for upgrading the organization's cybersecurity strategy based on the latest assessment findings.

This stage is also when the security manager, security team, and business stakeholders come together and collaborate, analyzing the issues identified during the previous assessment step. This group, as a committee, will look at the security program, along with any currently identified challenges such as a lack of executive support, incomplete inventories, audit gaps, or incorrect security processes. By the end of this process, they will have created a list of prioritized issues that will need to be addressed.

The security manager will then be tasked to review the prioritized list, ensuring that the issues are correctly ranked based on their impact on business operations, increased risk exposure to the business, or required by regulations or compliance regimes. Once this review is completed, you will want to identify low-hanging fruit and score some early wins to build trust in your security program. You can then build a long-term strategy by taking the prioritized list of issues and weighing them against the current resources that your security program has available to remediate them.

As you can imagine, you will not have enough funds or people to do everything, so it will be incumbent on you to break the list up over a specific timeline (1-3 years) and use it as a roadmap for improvement. In the past, I have taken this roadmap and used it to create my security budget based on the remediation projects it contained. I have found that linking the strategic plan and security budget to how you will provide new services for stakeholders provides an understanding of the security program's value. With this value proposition in hand, we can now proceed to the fifth and final step, communicating.

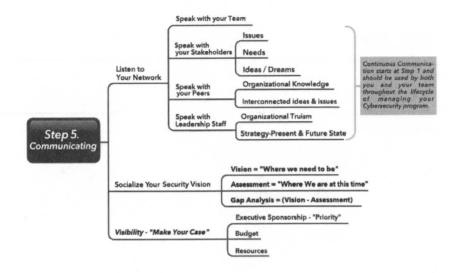

Step 5 Communicating

5. Communicating

We have collected all our notes and findings and have developed our new budget and strategic vision for upgrading the organization's cybersecurity program. This strategy, with its prioritized list of security issues, will now need to be socialized. As the security manager, you will need support for implementing the changes that many of your initiatives will require the business to make. Change is not accepted readily by most employees, so this support is crucial. To begin, I would start by first communicating the findings of the assessment. Describe where you are presently from an overall cyber perspective, and then add your vision of where you want to go.

Explain how your proposed initiatives will close the identified gaps and resolve open issues. Make sure employees understand the business value in delivering these outcomes. Expect in this final phase that you will do a lot of talking and hosting events with employees to let them know who you are and what you are doing in your security program. Help them understand the value you bring to the business. With that said, make sure to also listen to your customers.

They will have good ideas to help you and your security team resolve issues. Be visible with employees and be an advocate for the security program and eventually they will accept you, and security will be on the way to becoming part of the business culture.

In the end, all of these steps take time, and they are a continuous process. As the SMB's security manager, you will be sifting through and collecting large amounts of information in assessing and building the company's cybersecurity program; it's OK to ask for help. I have found it is good to remember you can't do it all immediately; use your team, reach out to peers for advice, and develop those relationships with stakeholders. They are your customers. I have found that working in cybersecurity is amazing. I thoroughly enjoy the challenges it brings, and I hope this final roadmap I have shared with you will help as you take on new challenges.

Chapter 22

What CEOs Should Know About the Security Manager Role and the Security Program?

In previous articles, books, and speeches, I have discussed the changing roles of the modern security executive and how the new job requirements of the security manager and their security teams are focused on providing risk management services to their company. Part of these earlier discussions with our community has focused on the threats facing businesses today and how security leaders should leverage technology, policy, and people to be more effective. However, there is still an executive leadership component I haven't touched on. That component is educating CEOs and leadership teams about the security executive role in whatever form it is employed, and on cybersecurity in general within businesses today. I believe the following points are critical for leadership to understand their enterprise security program, the security executive role, and the business value of an adequately resourced cybersecurity program.

1. Information Security is not an Information Technology (IT) problem

Cybersecurity in its fundamental essence is about data and risk. It's about the use of technology to access, acquire, process, manipulate, or retire data. Yes, cybersecurity does use technology to manage the risk exposure for enterprise data. However, it also applies policies, security controls, frameworks, and people in this endeavor as well. I view cybersecurity and the job of the security manager and security teams as providing enterprise risk management services to their business. The security manager's role is not to own the business's risk but to understand the business's strategic goals, its operations, its revenue processes, and how it uses technology to compete, and therefore be in a better position to help the business manage its business risks. With this insight, security leaders have visibility into the risk exposure of the business and can make recommendations on how to manage risk. The company, which owns the risk, makes the final decision on how the risk will and should be managed, and the security manager implements and monitors protective strategies according to their direction and established risk tolerances. This view is very different from the CIO's, whose role is to deliver efficient enterprise IT services to support the business in achieving its strategic goals. As you can see, both use technology, but from very different viewpoints. Therefore, I believe whenever possible, security managers should be peers to IT managers, so the business gets a more in-depth and balanced view of its technical and operations-based risk exposures.

2. Security is a risk management problem

As I mentioned above, cybersecurity is about risk. It's about how technology is used and the data it creates. It is about who has access to that technology and data; are they authorized, do we have records of access granted and utilized, and which third parties have access? It's about having a methodical process based on a standard framework to measure risk, equate it to the financial impact to services, remediate the issues we discover, and then decide how to manage and monitor the remaining risks. This reduces the impact of these risks on the organization's strategic operations. To do this effectively, I say to CEOs that your security manager must have experience in multiple domains to understand the interrelationships of disparate technologies, work processes, compliance requirements, and business operations. Then with this insight, they should be able to convert this highly technical view on hazards to the business into a discussion on impact to services and customer operations. This is not a natural skill. However, it is one learned from years of experience, and it is the business value that a mature security manager brings to a company of any size, from SMB to a Fortune 500 corporation.

3. Security doesn't bring value in a box

An organization's security program should not be pushed to the side and constrained. It needs to be visible to everyone in the organization, and employees should know both the security manager and the security team. A mature security program is one that is integrated across departments, assisting with risk management issues and looking for vulnerabilities. A seasoned security program is one in which all employees know who they can call when they have problems or need to report something anomalous about their computer. Security by its nature is about data and technology that crosses all aspects of a business, and the program and team that manages it needs to be involved and empowered to work cross-functionally and aid where needed. I have seen numerous places where almost no one knows who oversees the security team, where they sit, or what services they provide. To me, this is a failure on security leadership for not evangelizing the value of security to the business, and it's a failure on the SMB's leadership team for not using this critical asset to its full potential.

4. The value of your security program is directly proportional to your support

Security doesn't just happen. SMBs need a security practitioner who is willing to take the manager role and knows how to build a program that is tuned to the business's needs. A company just hiring a security manager hasn't protected the business by that act alone. This crucial role needs to be empowered. When the business engages its security leader and empowers them to envision a strategic roadmap and then provides the resources for them to build their program, they are investing in their future by building resiliency into their strategic operations. I believe an engaged security manager and security team offers the business the capability to be innovative in a more secure environment. This will enable it to increase its competitiveness at reduced costs and risk.

5. Security is about culture

The security manager, security team, and security program are collectively change agents. Security and its many controls and initiatives at times will be about changing the corporate culture for the betterment of the company. The CEO should publicly support the security manager and their efforts. Typically, I like to have something like a security charter that states that the security program has the support of executive leadership to make changes and manage the risk of the organization. Of course, it is then incumbent on the security manager to craft the programs and policies the company needs, evangelize the worth of these programs and policies, and then work with peers to implement them with support across the company. I have never worked anywhere in my 20+ years in IT or security where I did not run into resistance from corporate culture. It will happen on at least one security project or new policy. Therefore, as a security leader, you must have executive leadership buy-in on the need for your role and the security program.

6. Security isn't a "one and done," it's a lifecycle

Cybersecurity is a lifecycle. As the SMB grows and technologies and work processes change to meet new business requirements, so does the company's risk exposure. It is this ebb and flow of strategy-technology-people-policy that demonstrates cybersecurity is a continuous process of inventory, assessment, scanning, remediation, and monitoring of risk. To the CEO this means just hiring a security manager doesn't make the business safe. That security manager will need to build a security program, implement the program, manage the program, and collect data to demonstrate its worth to the company. It is a continuous process and to do it efficiently, the CEO and leadership team need to partner with their security manager. They need to understand and accept the security manager as a strategic asset or business executive who may not provide a revenue stream but will enhance the operations of other revenue-generating units and will help the leadership team sleep better at night.

7. Security isn't sexy, but customers will appreciate the business that has good security

With so many new threats and breaches reported nightly on the news, cybersecurity is becoming the corporate program that companies are expected to fund and use to protect their customers. Cybersecurity is also now being mandated by many regulations such as GLBA, CCPA, and GDPR, and these regulations carry hefty financial penalties. To do cybersecurity correctly, businesses need a security executive who is in tune with the company and its operations, and who understands the breadth of its strategic plans. This means that executive leadership will have to spend the time to make sure their security leader is educated on the business environment of the company. I have personally seen this done, where CISOs were assigned mentors from different business units to help them understand business operations. I have also seen businesses send their security manager to school for formal business education. What is important is that with this context into how businesses operate, the security manager can then build a competent security program that incorporates both the company's business needs and technical environments so they can better manage the organization's risk portfolio. Again, this is hard work that executive leadership must be a part of so that the security program is aligned with what the organization needs to be resilient and manage its risks. The result will be a security program that can better handle incidents and reduce their impact on customers and corporate operations.

8. Security is about discipline; the basics need to be done right, consistently

My final note is that cybersecurity is a field of numerous disciplines managed by frameworks and security controls. In this process, policies and work procedures are created that need to be followed methodically. Many of these procedures and guidelines are mundane and can be mind-numbing at best. With that said, if they are not completed, then security controls break down, and incidents soon follow. This scenario is the context behind the term "cyber-hygiene." It is implementing basic security procedures and then actually doing them every day, in the same manner, to manage risk and protect the business. This is an example of the discipline a mature security program must follow, and the SMB's security manager must lead, to keep the company secure. Both (program and manager) need executive leadership support to mature.

As I conclude this chapter, please understand that this is by no means everything a CEO or executive leadership team should know about their security manager role or their company's security program. My goal with this chapter is to start the conversation and hopefully provide a window into the security manager's world so that CEOs and executive teams can see why it is important that they support their security manager and that in the process their SMB will be better for it.

Conclusion

I enjoyed collecting these twenty-two articles and updating them for this book. After working with many startups and small businesses over the last several years, I frequently saw their security personnel struggling with how to protect their companies. This struggle was the spark for this book. It rolled around in my head late at night, keeping me up until I finally got busy and started to assemble all of the pieces.

I love our community and the amazing patchwork of people, cultures, businesses, and technologies that work together to form the cybersecurity discipline and career field many of us enjoy. This is why I wanted to focus on security professionals who are struggling to protect small and medium businesses. Many of you are working and leading security programs with minimal resources and support, so I wanted to provide this guidebook to help you grow as a professional.

I truly hope this book has provided some value to you and at least has you thinking about where you can make improvements to your security program. As a security manager it is important to lead and manage your teams and I again hope I have given you some insight into how to improve daily team and security services. With that said, good luck and blessings to you and your teams. If you need anything don't hesitate to ask for help, our community is all around you and we are available to assist you.

Appendix A: Glossary of Terms and Acronyms

Two primary sources of definitions for terms and acronyms related to cybersecurity were used in this book:

(1) NIST Interagency/Internal Report (NIST-IR) #7298 R2 (May 2013) *
https://nvlpubs.nist.gov/nistpubs/ir/2013/nist.ir.7298r2.pdf

(2) Committee on National Security Systems Instructions (CNSSI) #4009 (April 2015) *

*Both sources are considered to be outdated and are being replaced with a new, online reference at
https://csrc.nist.gov/glossary

While some of the following terms or phrases may be defined in other places, for this book, they have the meanings and definitions provided below.

Access Control List (ACL)	Concerning a computer file system, an ACL is a list of permissions attached to an object. An ACL specifies which users or system processes are granted access to objects, as well as what operations are allowed on given objects.
Accountability	Every individual who works with an information system should have specific responsibilities for that information's protection.
Adequate Security	Security commensurate with the risk resulting from the loss, misuse, or unauthorized access to or modification of information.

Administrative Account	An administrator account is a user account that allows you to make changes that will affect other users. Administrators can change security settings, install software and hardware, and access all files on the computer. Administrators can also make changes to other user accounts.
Administrative Access Controls	Administrative controls define the human factors of security. It involves all levels of personnel within an organization and determines which users have access to what resources and information by such means as Training and awareness. Disaster preparedness and recovery plans.
Advanced Persistent Threat (APT)	An adversary that possesses sophisticated levels of expertise and significant resources which allow it to create opportunities to achieve its objectives by using multiple attack vectors (e.g., cyber, physical, and deception). These objectives typically include establishing and extending footholds within the information technology infrastructure of the targeted organizations for purposes of exfiltrating information, undermining or impeding critical aspects of a mission, program, or organization; or positioning itself to carry out these objectives in the future.
Anomaly-Based Detection	An anomaly-based intrusion detection system is an intrusion detection system for detecting both network and computer intrusions and misuse by monitoring system activity and classifying it as either normal or anomalous.
Assessment	See *Security Control Assessment.*
Assessor	See *Security Control Assessor.*

Asset	In information security, computer security, and network security, an asset is any data, device, or another component of the environment that supports information-related activities.
Assurance	The measure of confidence that the security features, practices, procedures, and architecture of an information system accurately mediates and enforces the security policy.
Assurance Case	A structured set of arguments and a body of evidence showing that an information system satisfies specific claims concerning a given quality attribute.
Audit Log	A chronological record of information system activities, including records of system accesses and operations performed in a given period.
Audit Record	An individual entry in an audit log related to an audited event.
Audit Reduction Tools	Preprocessors designed to reduce the volume of audit records to facilitate a manual review. Before a security review, these tools can remove many audit records known to have little security significance. These tools generally remove records generated by specified classes of events, such as records generated by nightly backups.
Audit Trail	A chronological record that reconstructs and examines the sequence of activities surrounding or leading to a specific operation, procedure, or event in a security-relevant transaction from inception to the final result.
Authentication	We are verifying the identity of a user, process, or device, often as a prerequisite to allowing access to resources in an information system.

Authenticator	The means used to confirm the identity of a user, processor, or device (e.g., user password or token).
Authenticity	The property of being genuine and being able to be verified and trusted; confidence in the validity of a transmission, a message, or message originator. See *Authentication.*
Authorization	A concept that directly relates to who has the right or privilege to access the information infrastructure. Access rights are determined by an information security plan that should be approved by the organization's legitimate authority or governing board.
Availability	You are ensuring timely and reliable access to and use of information.
Baseline Configuration	A documented set of specifications for an information system, or a configuration item within a system, that has been formally reviewed and agreed on at a given point in time, and which can be changed only through change control procedures.
Blacklisting	The process used to identify: (i) software programs that are not authorized to execute on an information system; or (ii) prohibited Universal Resource Locators (URL)/websites.
Boundary Protection	Monitoring and control of communications at the external boundary of an information system to prevent and detect malicious and other unauthorized communications, through the use of boundary protection devices (e.g., gateways, routers, firewalls, guards, encrypted tunnels).

Boundary Protection Device	A device with appropriate mechanisms that: (i) facilitates the adjudication of different interconnected system security policies (e.g., controlling the flow of information into or out of an interconnected system); or (ii) provides information system boundary protection.
Business Continuity (BC)	Business continuity planning is the process of creating systems of prevention and recovery to deal with potential threats to a company. In addition to prevention, the goal is to enable ongoing operations before and during the execution of disaster recovery.
Business Impact Analysis (B.I.A.)	Business impact analysis (BIA) is a systematic process to determine and evaluate the potential effects of an interruption to critical business operations as a result of a disaster, accident, or emergency.
C.I.A.	Confidentiality, Integrity, Availability: This is known as the Triad of Cybersecurity; the ultimate goal of security measures and controls is to protect information assets' *Confidentiality* (only those authorized to access the information can access it), *Integrity* (assurance that the information has not been altered or deleted), and *Availability* (the information is accessible by authorized individuals when it is needed).
Center for Internet Security (CIS)	The Center for Internet Security (CIS) is a 501(c)(3) nonprofit organization formed in October 2000. Its mission is to "identify, develop, validate, promote, and sustain best practice solutions for cyber defense and build and lead communities to enable an environment of trust in cyberspace."

Central Management	The organization-wide management and implementation of selected security controls and related processes. Central management includes planning, implementing, assessing, authorizing, and monitoring the organization-defined, centrally managed security controls and processes.
Chief Information Officer	Executive responsible for providing advice and assistance to the executive leadership of an organization or other senior management personnel to ensure that information technology is acquired and information resources are managed in a manner that is consistent with laws, directives, policies, regulations, and priorities established by the organization; Developing, maintaining, and facilitating the implementation of a sound and integrated information technology architecture for the organization; and promoting the effective and efficient design and operation of all major information resources management processes for the organization.
Chief Information Security Officer	A chief information security officer (CISO) is the senior-level executive within an organization responsible for establishing and maintaining the enterprise vision, strategy, and program to ensure information assets and technologies are adequately protected. The CISO directs staff in identifying, developing, implementing, and maintaining processes across the enterprise to reduce information and information technology (IT) risks. They respond to incidents, establish appropriate standards and controls, manage security technologies, and direct the establishment and implementation of policies and procedures.

Chief Privacy Officer	A chief privacy officer (CPO) is a corporate executive charged with developing and implementing policies designed to protect employee and customer data from unauthorized access. Other elements of the CPO job include maintaining a comprehensive and current knowledge of both corporate operations and privacy laws, as well as communicating details of the company's privacy policy to staff and customers alike. The CPO is typically the organization's point person for media and other external inquiries about privacy-related matters.
Cloud Computing	Cloud computing is the on-demand availability of computer system resources, especially data storage and computing power, without direct active management by the user. The term is generally used to describe data centers available to many users over the Internet.
Commodity Service	An information system service (e.g., telecommunications service) provided by a commercial service provider typically to a large and diverse set of consumers.
Common Carrier	In a telecommunications context, a telecommunications company that holds itself out to the public for hire to provide communications transmission services. Note: In the United States, such companies are usually subject to regulation by federal and state regulatory commissions.
Common Control	A security control that is inheritable by one or more organizational information systems. See *Security Control Inheritance*.
Common Control Provider	An organizational employee responsible for the development, implementation, assessment, and monitoring of common controls (i.e., security controls inheritable by information systems).

Common Criteria	Governing document that provides a comprehensive, rigorous method for specifying security function and assurance requirements for products and systems.
Common Secure Configuration	A recognized standardized, an established benchmark that stipulates specific secure configuration settings for a given information technology platform.
Compensating Security Controls	The security controls employed in place of the recommended controls in the security control baselines described in frameworks such as NIST Special Publication 800-53 or ISO 27001 that provide equivalent or comparable protection for an information system or organization.
Confidentiality	We are preserving authorized restrictions on information access and disclosure, including means for protecting personal privacy and proprietary information.
Configuration Control	Process for controlling modifications to hardware, firmware, software, and documentation to protect the information system against improper modifications before, during, and after system implementation.
Configuration Item	An aggregation of information system components that is designated for configuration management and treated as a single entity in the configuration management process.
Configuration Management	A collection of activities focused on establishing and maintaining the integrity of information technology products and information systems, through control of processes for initializing, changing, and monitoring the configurations of those products and systems throughout the system development life cycle.

Configuration Settings
: The set of parameters that can be changed in hardware, software, or firmware that affect the security posture or functionality of the information system.

Controlled Area
: Any area or space for which an organization has confidence that the physical and procedural protections provided are sufficient to meet the requirements established for protecting the information or information system.

Controlled Interface
: A boundary with a set of mechanisms that enforces the security policies and controls the flow of information between interconnected information systems.

Countermeasures
: Actions, devices, procedures, techniques, or other measures that reduce the vulnerability of an information system. Synonymous with security controls and safeguards.

Covert Channel Analysis
: Determination of the extent to which the security policy model and subsequent lower-level program descriptions may allow unauthorized access to information.

Covert Storage Channel
: Covert channel involving the direct or indirect writing to a storage location by one process and the direct or indirect reading of the storage location by another process. Covert storage channels typically involve a finite resource (e.g., sectors on a disk) that is shared by two subjects at different security levels.

Covert Timing Channel
: A covert channel in which one process signals information to another process by modulating its use of system resources (e.g., central processing unit time) in such a way that this manipulation affects the real response time observed by the second process.

Credentials or Electronic Credentials	A credential is an attestation of qualification, competence, or authority issued to an individual by a third party with a relevant or de facto authority or assumed competence to do so.
Critical Security Controls (CSC)	The CIS Critical Security Controls are a recommended set of actions for cyber defense that provide specific and actionable ways to stop today's most pervasive and dangerous attacks. A principal benefit of the Controls is that they prioritize and focus a smaller number of actions with high pay-off results.
Cross-Domain Solution	A form of controlled interface that provides the ability to manually or automatically access or transfer information between different security domains.
CSF	Cybersecurity Framework: this refers to the NIST "Framework for Improving Critical Infrastructure Cybersecurity" ver. 1.1, issued in April 2018.
CSIRT	Computer Security Incident Response Team - a group of IT professionals that provides an organization with services and support surrounding the prevention, management and coordination of potential cybersecurity-related emergencies.
Cyber Attack	An attack, via cyberspace, targeting an enterprise's use of cyberspace for the purpose of disrupting, disabling, destroying, or maliciously controlling a computing environment/infrastructure; or destroying the integrity of the data or stealing controlled information.

Cyber Hygiene	Cyber hygiene is a reference to the practices and steps that users of computers and other devices take to maintain system health and improve online security. These practices are often part of a routine to ensure the safety of identity and other details that could be stolen or corrupted.
Cybersecurity	Computer security, cybersecurity, or information technology security is the protection of computer systems from the theft of or damage to their hardware, software, or electronic data, as well as from the disruption or misdirection of the services they provide.
Cyberspace	A global domain within the information environment consisting of the interdependent network of information systems infrastructures, including the Internet, telecommunications networks, computer systems, and embedded processors and controllers.
Data Mining/Harvesting	An analytical process that attempts to find correlations or patterns in large data sets for data or knowledge discovery.
Defense-in-Breadth	A planned, systematic set of multidisciplinary activities that seek to identify, manage and reduce risk of exploitable vulnerabilities at every stage of the system, network, or subcomponent life cycle (system, network, or product design and development; manufacturing; packaging; assembly; system integration; distribution; operations; maintenance; and retirement).
Defense-in-Depth	Information security strategy integrating people, technology, and operations capabilities to establish variable barriers across multiple layers and missions of the organization.

Developer	A general term that includes: (i) developers or manufacturers of information systems, system components, or information system services; (ii) systems integrators; (iii) vendors; and (iv) product resellers. Development of systems, components, or services can occur internally within organizations (i.e., in-house development) or through external entities.
Digital Media	A form of electronic media where data are stored in digital (as opposed to analog) form.
Disaster Recovery (DR)	Disaster Recovery involves a set of policies, tools, and procedures to enable the recovery or continuation of vital technology infrastructure and systems following a natural or human-induced disaster.
Discretionary Access Control	An access control policy that is enforced over all subjects and objects in an information system where the policy specifies that a subject that has been granted access to information can do one or more of the following: (i) pass the information to other subjects or objects; (ii) grant its privileges to other subjects; (iii) change security attributes on subjects, objects, information systems, or system components; (iv) choose the security attributes to be associated with newly-created or revised objects; or (v) change the rules governing access control. Mandatory access controls restrict this capability.
Domain	An environment or context that includes a set of system resources and a set of system entities that have the right to access the resources as defined by a common security policy, security model, or security architecture. See *Security Domain*.

Enterprise	An organization with a defined mission/goal and a defined boundary, using information systems to execute that mission, and with responsibility for managing its risks and performance. An enterprise may consist of all or some of the following business aspects: acquisition, program management, financial management (e.g., budgets), human resources, security, and information systems, information, and mission management. See *Organization*.
Enterprise Architecture	A strategic information asset base, which defines the mission; the information necessary to perform the mission; the technologies necessary to perform the mission; and the transitional processes for implementing new technologies in response to changing mission needs; and includes a baseline architecture; a target architecture; and a sequencing plan.
Environment of Operation	The physical surroundings in which information system processes, stores, and transmits information.
Event	Any observable occurrence in an information system.
Exfiltration	The unauthorized transfer of information from an information system.
External Information System (or Component)	An information system or component of an information system that is outside of the boundary established by the organization and for which the organization typically has no direct control over the application of required security controls or the assessment of security control effectiveness.

External Information System Service	An information system service that is implemented outside of the authorization boundary of the organizational information system (i.e., a service that is used by, but not a part of, the organizational information system) and for which the organization typically has no direct control over the application of required security controls or the assessment of security control effectiveness.
External Information System Service Provider	A provider of external information system services to an organization through a variety of consumer-producer relationships, including but not limited to: joint ventures; business partnerships; outsourcing arrangements (i.e., through contracts, interagency agreements, lines of business arrangements); licensing agreements; or supply chain exchanges.
External Network	A network not controlled by the organization.
Failover	The capability to switch over automatically (typically without human intervention or warning) to a redundant or standby information system upon the failure or abnormal termination of the previously active system.
Fair Information Practice Principles	Principles that are widely accepted in the United States and internationally as a general framework for privacy and that are reflected in various federal and international laws and policies. In some organizations, the principles serve as the basis for analyzing privacy risks and determining appropriate mitigation strategies.

FIPS	Federal Information Processing Standard - are a set of standards that describe document processing, encryption algorithms, and other information technology standards for use within non-military government agencies and by government contractors and vendors who work with the agencies.
FIPS-Validated Cryptography	A cryptographic module validated by the Cryptographic Module Validation Program (CMVP) to meet requirements specified in FIPS Publication 140-2 (as amended). As a prerequisite to CMVP validation, the cryptographic module is required to employ a cryptographic algorithm implementation that has successfully passed validation testing by the Cryptographic Algorithm
	Validation Program (CAVP). See *NSA-Approved Cryptography*.
Firmware	Computer programs and data stored in hardware - typically in read-only memory (ROM) or programmable read-only memory (PROM) - such that the programs and data cannot be dynamically written or modified during execution of the programs.
Hardware	The physical components of an information system. See *Software* and *Firmware*.
Hybrid Security Control	A security control that is implemented in an information system in part as a common control and part as a system-specific control. See *Common Control* and *System-Specific Security Control*.
Identity and Access Management (IAM)	Identity management, also known as identity and access management, is a framework of policies and technologies for ensuring that the proper people in an enterprise have the appropriate access to technology resources.

Identity-Based Access Control	Access control based on the identity of the user (typically relayed as a characteristic of the process acting on behalf of that user) where access authorizations to specific objects are assigned based on user identity.
Impact	The effect on organizational operations, organizational assets, individuals, other organizations, or the Nation (including the national security interests of the United States) of a loss of confidentiality, integrity, or availability of information or an information system.
Impact Value	Sometimes referred to as "Severity," this refers to the monetary value a business assigns to the tangible and intangible business impacts if a particular asset is compromised. Impacts include but are not limited to, direct monetary loss (theft), loss of revenue, loss of business reputation, loss of customers, and the costs to halt and remediate a cyber-attack.
Incident	An occurrence that actually or potentially jeopardizes the confidentiality, integrity, or availability of an information system or the information the system processes, stores, or transmits or that constitutes a violation or imminent threat of violation of security policies, security procedures, or acceptable use policies.
Incident Response (IR)	Incident response is an organized approach to addressing and managing the aftermath of a security breach or cyberattack, also known as an IT incident, computer incident, or security incident. Incident response is initiated in teams by an organization's security team leadership.

Industrial Control System	An information system used to control industrial processes such as manufacturing, product handling, production, and distribution. Industrial control systems include supervisory control and data acquisition (SCADA) systems used to control geographically dispersed assets, as well as distributed control systems (DCSs) and smaller control systems using programmable logic controllers to control localized processes.
Information	Any communication or representation of knowledge such as facts, data, or opinions in any medium or form, including textual, numerical, graphic, cartographic, narrative, or audiovisual. An instance of an information type.
Information Leakage	The intentional or unintentional release of information to an untrusted environment.
Information Owner	Official with statutory or operational authority for specified information and responsibility for establishing the controls for its generation, collection, processing, dissemination, and disposal.
Information Resources	Information and related resources, such as personnel, equipment, funds, and information technology.
Information Security	The protection of information and information systems from unauthorized access, use, disclosure, disruption, modification, or destruction to provide confidentiality, integrity, and availability.
Information Security Architecture	An embedded, integral part of the enterprise architecture that describes the structure and behavior for an enterprise's security processes, information security systems, personnel, and organizational subunits, showing their alignment with the enterprise's mission and strategic plans.

Information Security Policy	An aggregate of directives, regulations, rules, and practices that prescribes how an organization manages, protects, and distributes information.
Information Security Program Plan	A formal document that provides an overview of the security requirements for an organization-wide information security program and describes the program management controls and common controls in place or planned for meeting those requirements.
Information Security Risk	The risk to organizational operations (including mission, functions, image, reputation), organizational assets, individuals, other organizations, and the Nation due to the potential for unauthorized access, use, disclosure, disruption, modification, or destruction of information or information systems.
Information Steward	An organizational employee with statutory or operational authority for specified information and responsibility for establishing the controls for its generation, collection, processing, dissemination, and disposal.
Information System	A discrete set of information resources organized for the collection, processing, maintenance, use, sharing, dissemination, or disposition of information.
Information System Component	A discrete, identifiable information technology asset (e.g., hardware, software, firmware) that represents a building block of an information system. Information system components include commercial information technology products.

Information System Owner	Individual responsible for the overall procurement, development, integration, modification, or operation and maintenance of an information system.
Information System Resilience	The ability of an information system to continue to: (i) operate under adverse conditions or stress, even if in a degraded or debilitated state while maintaining essential operational capabilities; and (ii) recover to an effective operational posture in a time frame consistent with mission needs.
Information System Security Officer	Individuals with assigned responsibility for maintaining the appropriate operational security posture for an information system or program.
Information System Service	A capability provided by an information system that facilitates information processing, storage, or transmission.
Information System-Related Security Risks	Risks that arise through the loss of confidentiality, integrity, or availability of information or information systems and that considers impacts to the organization (including assets, mission, functions, image, or reputation), individuals, other organizations, and the Nation. See *Risk*.
Information Technology	Any equipment or interconnected system or subsystem of equipment that is used in the automatic acquisition, storage, manipulation, management, movement, control, display, switching, interchange, transmission, or reception of data or information by the organization.
Information Technology Product	See *Information System Component*.

Information Type	A specific category of information (e.g., privacy, medical, proprietary, financial, investigative, contractor-sensitive, security management) defined by an organization or in some instances, by a specific law, directive, policy, or regulation.
Insider	Any person with authorized access to any internal organizational resource, to include personnel, facilities, information, equipment, networks, or systems.
Insider Threat	The threat that an insider will use her/his authorized access, wittingly or unwittingly, to harm the security of their organization. This threat can include damage through industrial espionage, unauthorized disclosure, access or theft of company proprietary information, or through the loss or degradation of departmental resources or capabilities.
Insider Threat Program	A coordinated group of capabilities under centralized management that is organized to detect and prevent the unauthorized disclosure of sensitive information.
Integrity	Guarding against improper information modification or destruction, and includes ensuring information non-repudiation and authenticity.
Internal Network	A network where: (i) the establishment, maintenance, and provisioning of security controls are under the direct control of organizational employees or contractors; or (ii) cryptographic encapsulation or similar security technology implemented between organization-controlled endpoints, provides the same effect (at least concerning confidentiality and integrity). An internal network is typically organization-owned, yet maybe organization-controlled while not being organization-owned.

Intrusion Detection System (IDS)	A security service that monitors and analyzes network or system events for finding, and providing real-time or near real-time warning of, attempts to access system resources in an unauthorized manner.
Intrusion Prevention System (IPS)	A system that can detect an intrusive activity and can also attempt to stop the activity, ideally before it reaches its targets.
Label	See *Security Label*.
Likelihood of Occurrence	Sometimes measured as the "Frequency of Occurrence," this refers to the probability of a particular vulnerability will be exploited by any particular threat, or how often a vulnerability will be exploited over one year.
Line of Business	The following process areas are common to many organizations: Procurement, Financial Management, Comptroller, Human Resources Management, Information Systems, Information Security, Training, Sales, and Product/Strategy.
Local Access	Access to an organizational information system by a user (or process acting on behalf of a user) communicating through a direct connection without the use of a network.
Logical Access Control System	An automated system that controls an individual's ability to access one or more computer system resources such as a workstation, network, application, or database. A logical access control system requires validation of an individual's identity through some mechanism such as a PIN, card, biometric, or other tokens. It can assign different access privileges to different persons depending on their roles and responsibilities in an organization.

Malicious Code	Software or firmware intended to perform an unauthorized process that will harm the confidentiality, integrity, or availability of an information system. A virus, worm, Trojan horse, or other code-based entity that infects a host. Spyware and some forms of adware are also examples of malicious code.
Malware	See *Malicious Code.*
Managed Interface	An interface within an information system that provides boundary protection capability using automated mechanisms or devices.
Mandatory Access Control	An access control policy that is uniformly enforced across all subjects and objects within the boundary of an information system. A subject that has been granted access to information is constrained from doing any of the following: (i) passing the information to unauthorized subjects or objects; (ii) granting its privileges to other subjects; (iii) changing one or more security attributes on subjects, objects, the information system, or system components; (iv) choosing the security attributes to be associated with newly-created or modified objects; or (v) changing the rules governing access control. Organization-defined subjects may explicitly be granted organization-defined privileges (i.e., they are trusted subjects) such that they are not limited by some or all of the above constraints.
Marking	See *Security Marking.*
Media	Physical devices or writing surfaces including, but not limited to, magnetic tapes, optical disks, magnetic disks, Large-Scale Integration (LSI) memory chips, and printouts (but not including display media) onto which information is recorded, stored or printed within an information system.

Metadata	Information describing the characteristics of data including, for example, structural metadata describing data structures (e.g., data format, syntax, and semantics) and descriptive metadata describing data contents (e.g., information security labels).
Mobile Code	Software programs or parts of programs obtained from remote information systems, transmitted across a network, and executed on a local information system without explicit installation or execution by the recipient.
Mobile Code Technologies	Software technologies that provide the mechanisms for the production and use of mobile code (e.g., Java, JavaScript, ActiveX, VBScript).
Mobile Device	A portable computing device that: (i) has a small form factor such that a single individual can easily carry it; (ii) is designed to operate without a physical connection (e.g., wirelessly transmit or receive information); (iii) possesses local, non-removable or removable data storage; and (iv) includes a self-contained power source. Mobile devices may also include voice communication capabilities, on-board sensors that allow the devices to capture information or built-in features for synchronizing local data with remote locations. Examples include smartphones, tablets, and E-readers.
Multifactor Authentication	Authentication using two or more different factors to achieve authentication. Factors include: (i) something you know (e.g., password/PIN); (ii) something you have (e.g., cryptographic identification device, token); or (iii) something you are (e.g., biometric). See *Authenticator*.

Multiple Security Levels	The capability of an information system that is trusted to contain and maintain separation between resources (particularly stored data) of different security domains.
Network	Information system(s) implemented with a collection of interconnected components. Such components may include routers, hubs, cabling, telecommunications controllers, key distribution centers, and technical control devices.
Network Access	Access to an information system by a user (or a process acting on behalf of a user) communicating through a network (e.g., local area network, wide area network, Internet).
Next-Generation Firewall (NGF or NGFW)	A next-generation firewall is a part of the third generation of firewall technology, combining a traditional firewall with other network device filtering functionalities, such as an application firewall using in-line deep packet inspection, an intrusion prevention system.
NIST	National Institute of Standards and Technology (within the U.S. Department of Commerce): This is the federal agency responsible for creating cybersecurity standards and guidelines, which are generally mandatory for all U.S. government agencies, as well as private companies under government contracts. Otherwise, the standards provide private businesses with a common set of security measures, most of which are mapped to other regulatory standards, such as HIPAA (Health Insurance Portability and Accountability Act) and PCI-DSS (Payment Card Industry Data Security Standards).
Nondiscretionary Access Control	See *Mandatory Access Control*.

Nonlocal Maintenance	Maintenance activities conducted by individuals communicating through a network, either an external network (e.g., the Internet) or an internal network.
Non-Organizational User	A user who is not organizational (including public users). Typically a 3rd party such as a vendor or trusted partner.
Non-repudiation	Protection against an individual falsely denying having performed a particular action. It provides the capability to determine whether a given individual took a particular action, such as creating information, sending a message, approving the information, and receiving a message.
Object	Passive information system-related entity (e.g., devices, files, records, tables, processes, programs, domains) containing or receiving information. Access to an object (by a subject) implies access to the information it contains. See *Subject*.
Operational Controls	The security controls (i.e., safeguards or countermeasures) for an information system that are primarily implemented and executed by people (as opposed to systems).
Operations Security	Systematic and proven process by which potential adversaries can be denied information about capabilities and intentions by identifying, controlling, and protecting generally non-sensitive evidence of the planning and execution of sensitive activities. The process involves five steps: identification of critical information, analysis of threats, analysis of vulnerabilities, assessment of risks, and application of appropriate countermeasures.

Organization	An entity of any size, complexity, or position within an organizational structure (e.g., a corporation, an agency, or, as appropriate, any of its operational elements).
Organizational User	An organizational employee or an individual, the organization, deems to have the equivalent status of an employee, including, for example, contractor, guest researcher, individual detailed from another organization. Policy and procedures for granting the equivalent status of employees to individuals may include need-to-know, relationship to the organization, and job function.
Overlay	A specification of security controls, control enhancements, supplemental guidance, and other supporting information employed during the tailoring process that is intended to complement (and further refine) security control baselines. The overlay specification may be more stringent or less stringent than the original security control baseline specification and can be applied to multiple information systems.
Penetration Testing	A test methodology in which assessors, typically working under specific constraints, attempt to circumvent or defeat the security features of an information system.
Personally Identifiable Information	Information which can be used to distinguish or trace the identity of an individual (e.g., name, social security number, biometric records, etc.) alone, or when combined with other personal or identifying information which is linked or linkable to a specific individual (e.g., date and place of birth, mother's maiden name, etc.).

Physical Access Control System	An automated system that manages the passage of people or assets through an opening(s) in a secure perimeter(s) based on a set of authorization rules.
Plan of Action and Milestones	A document that identifies tasks needing to be accomplished. It details resources required to accomplish the elements of the plan, any milestones in meeting the tasks, and scheduled completion dates for the milestones.
Portable Storage Device	An information system component that can be inserted into and removed from an information system, and that is used to store data or information (e.g., text, video, audio, or image data). Such components are typically implemented on magnetic, optical, or solid-state devices (e.g., floppy disks, compact/digital video disks, flash/thumb drives, external hard disk drives, and flash memory cards/drives that contain non-volatile memory).
Potential Impact	The loss of confidentiality, integrity, or availability could be expected to have: (i) a *limited* adverse effect; (ii) a *serious* adverse effect; or (iii) a *severe* or *catastrophic* adverse effect on organizational operations, organizational assets, or individuals.
Privacy Impact Assessment	An analysis of how information is handled: (i) to ensure handling conforms to applicable legal, regulatory, and policy requirements regarding privacy; (ii) to determine the risks and effects of collecting, maintaining, and disseminating information in identifiable form in an electronic information system; and (iii) to examine and evaluate protections and alternative processes for handling information to mitigate potential privacy risks.
Privileged Account	An information system account with authorizations of a privileged user.

Privileged Command	A human-initiated command executed on an information system involving the control, monitoring, or administration of the system, including security functions and associated security-relevant information.
Privileged User	A user that is authorized (and therefore, trusted) to perform security-relevant functions that ordinary users are not authorized to perform.
Protective Distribution System	Wireline or fiber-optic system that includes adequate safeguards or countermeasures (e.g., acoustic, electric, electromagnetic, and physical) to permit its use for the transmission of unencrypted information.
Provenance	The records are describing the possession of, and changes to, components, component processes, information, systems, organization, and organizational processes. Provenance enables all changes to the baselines of components, component processes, information, systems, organizations, and organizational processes, to be reported to specific actors, functions, locales, or activities.
Public Key Infrastructure	The framework and services that provide for the generation, production, distribution, control, accounting, and destruction of public-key certificates. Components include the personnel, policies, processes, server platforms, software, and workstations used to administer certificates and public-private key pairs, including the ability to issue, maintain, recover, and revoke public key certificates.
Purge	Rendering sanitized data unrecoverable by laboratory attack methods.

Reciprocity

Mutual agreement among participating organizations to accept each other's security assessments to reuse information system resources or to accept each other's assessed security posture to share information.

Records

The recordings (automated or manual) of evidence of activities performed or resulted achieved (e.g., forms, reports, test results), which serve as a basis for verifying that the organization and the information system are performing as intended. Also used to refer to units of related data fields (i.e., groups of data fields that can be accessed by a program and that contain the complete set of information on particular items).

Red Team Exercise

An exercise, reflecting real-world conditions, that is conducted as a simulated adversarial attempt to compromise organizational missions or business processes to provide a comprehensive assessment of the security capability of the information system and organization.

Reference Monitor

A set of design requirements on a reference validation mechanism, which as a key component of an operating system, enforces an access control policy over all subjects and objects. A reference validation mechanism must be: (i) always invoked (i.e., complete mediation); (ii) tamperproof; and (iii) small enough to be subject to analysis and tests, the completeness of which can be assured (i.e., verifiable).

Remote Access

Access to an organizational information system by a user (or a process acting on behalf of a user) communicating through an external network (e.g., the Internet).

Remote Maintenance

Maintenance activities conducted by individuals communicating through an external network (e.g., the Internet).

Resilience   See *Information System Resilience.*

Risk   A measure of the extent to which a potential
                                    circumstance or event threatens an entity, and
                                    typically a function of (i) the adverse impacts
                                    that would arise if the circumstance or event
                                    occurs; and (ii) the likelihood of occurrence.

                                    Information system-related security risks are
                                    those risks that arise from the loss of
                                    confidentiality, integrity, or availability of
                                    information or information systems and reflect
                                    the potential adverse impacts to organizational
                                    operations (including mission, functions, brand
                                    image, or reputation), organizational assets,
                                    individuals, other organizations, and partners.

Risk Assessment   The process of identifying risks to
                                    organizational operations (including mission,
                                    functions, image, reputation), organizational
                                    assets, individuals, other organizations, and
                                    partners, resulting from the operation of an
                                    information system.

                                    Part of risk management incorporates threat
                                    and vulnerability analyses and considers
                                    mitigations provided by security controls
                                    planned or in place. Synonymous with risk
                                    analysis.

Risk Executive (Function)

An individual or group within an organization that helps to ensure that: (i) security risk-related considerations for individual information systems, to include the authorization decisions for those systems, are viewed from an organization-wide perspective concerning the overall strategic goals and objectives of the organization in carrying out its missions and business functions; and (ii) managing risk from individual information systems is consistent across the organization, reflects organizational risk tolerance and is considered along with other organizational risks affecting mission/business success.

Risk Management

The program and supporting processes to manage information security risk to organizational operations (including mission, functions, brand image, reputation), organizational assets, individuals, other organizations, and partners, and includes: (i) establishing the context for risk-related activities; (ii) assessing risk; (iii) responding to risk once determined; and (iv) monitoring risk over time.

Risk Mitigation

Prioritizing, evaluating, and implementing the appropriate risk-reducing controls/countermeasures recommended from the risk management process.

Risk Monitoring

Maintaining ongoing awareness of an organization's risk environment, risk management program, and associated activities to support risk decisions.

Risk Response

Accepting, avoiding, mitigating, sharing, or transferring risk to organizational operations (i.e., mission, functions, brand image, or reputation), organizational assets, individuals, other organizations, or partners.

Risk Management Plan (RMP) | A risk management plan is a document that a project manager prepares to foresee risks, estimate impacts, and define responses to risks. It also contains a risk assessment matrix. A risk is "an uncertain event or condition that, if it occurs, has a positive or negative effect on a project's objectives.

Role-Based Access Control | Access control based on user roles (i.e., a collection of access authorizations a user receives based on an explicit or implicit assumption of a given role). Role permissions may be inherited through a role hierarchy and typically reflect the permissions needed to perform defined functions within an organization. A given role may apply to a single individual or several individuals.

Safeguards | Protective measures prescribed to meet the security requirements (i.e., confidentiality, integrity, and availability) specified for an information system. Safeguards may include security features, management constraints, personnel security, and security of physical structures, areas, and devices. Synonymous with security controls and countermeasures.

Sanitization | Actions were taken to render data written on media unrecoverable by both ordinary and, for some forms of sanitization, extraordinary means. The process of removing information from media such that data recovery is not possible. It includes removing all data classification labels, markings, and activity logs.

Scoping Considerations	A part of tailoring guidance providing organizations with specific considerations on the applicability and implementation of security controls in the security control baseline. Areas of consideration include policy/regulatory, technology, physical infrastructure, system component allocation, operational/environmental, public access, scalability, common control, and security objective.
Security	A condition that results from the establishment and maintenance of protective measures that enable an enterprise to perform its mission or critical functions despite risks posed by threats to its use of information systems. Protective measures may involve a combination of deterrence, avoidance, prevention, detection, recovery, and correction that should form part of the enterprise's risk management approach.
Security Assessment	See *Security Control Assessment*.
Security Assessment Plan	The objectives for the security control assessment and a detailed roadmap of how to conduct such an assessment.
Security Assurance	See *Assurance*.
Security Attribute	An abstraction representing the basic properties or characteristics of an entity for safeguarding information; typically associated with internal data structures (e.g., records, buffers, files) within the information system and used to enable the implementation of access control and flow control policies, reflect special dissemination, handling or distribution instructions, or support other aspects of the information security policy.
Security Authorization	See *Authorization*.

Security Authorization Boundary	See *Authorization Boundary*.
Security Capability	A combination of mutually-reinforcing security controls (i.e., safeguards and countermeasures) implemented by technical means (i.e., functionality in hardware, software, and firmware), physical means (i.e., physical devices and protective measures), and procedural means (i.e., procedures performed by individuals).
Security Category	The characterization of information or an information system based on an assessment of the potential impact that a loss of confidentiality, integrity, or availability of such information or information system would have on organizational operations, organizational assets, individuals, other organizations, and partners.
Security Control	A safeguard or countermeasure prescribed for an information system or an organization designed to protect the confidentiality, integrity, and availability of its information and to meet a set of defined security requirements.
Security Control Assessment	The testing or evaluation of security controls to determine the extent to which the controls are implemented correctly, operating as intended, and producing the desired outcome for meeting the security requirements for an information system or organization.
Security Control Assessor	The individual, group, or organization responsible for conducting a security control assessment.
Security Control Baseline	The set of minimum security controls that provides a starting point for establishing a level of acceptable risk as defined by the organization.

Security Control Enhancement	Augmentation of security control to (i) build in additional, but related, functionality to the control; (ii) increase the strength of the control; or (iii) add assurance to the control.
Security Control Inheritance	A situation in which an information system or application receives protection from security controls (or portions of security controls) that are developed, implemented, assessed, authorized, and monitored by entities other than those responsible for the system or application; entities either internal or external to the organization where the system or application resides. See *Common Control*.
Security Control Overlay	See *Overlay*.
Security Domain	A domain that implements a security policy and is administered by a single entity.
Security Functionality	The security-related features, functions, mechanisms, services, procedures, and architectures implemented within organizational information systems or the environments in which those systems operate.
Security Functions	The hardware, software, or firmware of the information system responsible for enforcing the system security policy and supporting the isolation of code and data on which the protection is based.
Security Impact Analysis	The analysis conducted by an organizational official to determine the extent to which changes to the information system have affected the security state of the system.
Security Incident	See *Incident*.
Security Label	The means used to associate a set of security attributes with a specific information object as part of the data structure for that object.

Security Marking   The means used to associate a set of
                           security attributes with objects in a
                           human-readable form, to enable
                           organizational process-based enforcement
                           of information security policies.

Security Objective   Confidentiality, integrity, or availability.

Security Plan   A formal document that provides an overview of
                           the security requirements for an information
                           system or an information security program and
                           describes the security controls in place or
                           planned for meeting those requirements.

                           See the *System Security Plan* or *Information
                           Security Program Plan*.

Security Policy   A set of criteria for the provision of security
                           services.

Security Policy Filter   A hardware or software component that
                           performs one or more of the following
                           functions: (i) content verification to ensure the
                           data type of the submitted content; (ii) content
                           inspection, analyzing the submitted content to
                           verify it complies with a defined policy (e.g.,
                           allowed vs. disallowed file constructs and
                           content portions); (iii) malicious content
                           checker that evaluates the content for malicious
                           code; (iv) suspicious activity checker that
                           evaluates or executes the content in a safe
                           manner, such as in a sandbox/detonation
                           chamber and monitors for suspicious activity; or
                           (v) content sanitization, cleansing, and
                           transformation, which modifies the submitted
                           content to comply with a defined policy.

Security Requirement

A requirement levied on an information system or an organization that is derived from applicable laws, directives, policies, standards, instructions, regulations, procedures, or mission/business needs to ensure the confidentiality, integrity, and availability of information that is being processed, stored, or transmitted.

Note: Security requirements can be used in a variety of contexts, from high-level policy-related activities to low-level implementation-related activities in system development and engineering disciplines.

Security Service

A capability that supports one, or more, of the security requirements (Confidentiality, Integrity, Availability). Examples of security services are key management, access control, and authentication.

Security-Relevant Information

Any information within the information system that can potentially impact the operation of security functions or the provision of security services in a manner that could fail to enforce the system security policy or maintain isolation of code and data.

Service-Oriented Architecture

A set of principles and methodologies for designing and developing software in the form of interoperable services. These services are well-defined business functions that are built as software components (i.e., discrete pieces of code or data structures) that can be reused for different purposes.

Signature-Based Detection

Signature-based detection is a process where a unique identifier is established about a known threat so that the threat can be identified in the future. In the case of a virus scanner, it may be a unique pattern of code that attaches to a file, or it may be as simple as the hash of a known bad file.

Software	Computer programs and associated data may be dynamically written or modified during execution.
Spam	The abuse of electronic messaging systems to indiscriminately send unsolicited bulk messages.
Spyware	Software that is secretly or surreptitiously installed into an information system to gather information on individuals or organizations without their knowledge; a type of malicious code.
Subject	Generally, an individual, process, or device causing the information to flow among objects or change to the system state. See *Object*.
Subsystem	A major subdivision or component of an information system consisting of information, information technology, and personnel that performs one or more specific functions.
Supplemental Guidance	Statements used to provide additional explanatory information for security controls or security control enhancements.
Supplementation	The process of adding security controls or control enhancements to a security control baseline as part of the tailoring process (during security control selection) to adequately meet the organization's risk management needs.
Supply Chain	Linked set of resources and processes between multiple tiers of developers that begins with the sourcing of products and services and extends through the design, development, manufacturing, processing, handling, and delivery of products and services to the acquirer.

Supply Chain Element — An information technology product or product component that contains programmable logic and that is critically important to the functioning of an information system.

System — See *Information System*.

System Security Plan — A formal document that provides an overview of the security requirements for an information system and describes the security controls in place or planned for meeting those requirements.

System-Specific Security Control — Security control for an information system that has not been designated as common security control or the portion of a hybrid control that is to be implemented within an information system.

Tailored Security Control Baseline — A set of security controls resulting from the application of tailoring guidance to a security control baseline. See *Tailoring*.

Tailoring — The process by which security control baselines are modified by:

(i) identifying and designating common controls; (ii) applying scoping considerations on the applicability and implementation of baseline controls; (iii) selecting compensating security controls; (iv) assigning specific values to organization-defined security control parameters; (v) supplementing baselines with additional security controls or control enhancements; and (vi) providing additional specification information for control implementation.

Technical Access Controls — The security controls (i.e., safeguards or countermeasures) for an information system that are primarily implemented and executed by the information system through mechanisms contained in the hardware, software, or firmware components of the system.

Threat	Any circumstance or event with the potential to adversely impact organizational operations (including mission, functions, image, or reputation), organizational assets, individuals, other organizations, or partners through an information system via unauthorized access, destruction, disclosure, modification of information, or denial of service.
Threat Assessment	Formal description and evaluation of the threat to an information system.
Threat Source	The intent and method targeted at the intentional exploitation of a vulnerability or a situation and method that may accidentally trigger a vulnerability. Synonymous with threat agent.
Trusted Path	A mechanism by which a user (through an input device) can communicate directly with the security functions of the information system with the necessary confidence to support the system security policy. This mechanism can only be activated by the user or the security functions of the information system and cannot be imitated by untrusted software.
Trustworthiness	The attribute of a person or enterprise that provides confidence to others of the qualifications, capabilities, and reliability of that entity to perform specific tasks and fulfill assigned responsibilities.
Trustworthiness (Information System)	The degree to which an information system (including the information technology components that are used to build the system) can be expected to preserve the confidentiality, integrity, and availability of the information being processed, stored, or transmitted by the system across the full range of threats.

User	Individual, or (system) process acting on behalf of an individual, authorized to access an information system.
Virtual Private Network	Protected information system links utilizing tunneling, security controls, and endpoint address translation giving the impression of a dedicated line.
Vulnerability	Weakness in an information system, system security procedures, internal controls, or implementation that could be exploited or triggered by a threat source.
Vulnerability Analysis	See *Vulnerability Assessment*.
Vulnerability Assessment	Systematic examination of an information system or product to determine the adequacy of security measures, identify security deficiencies, provide data from which to predict the effectiveness of proposed security measures, and confirm the adequacy of such measures after implementation.
Whitelisting	The process used to identify: (i) software programs that are authorized to execute on an information system; or (ii) authorized Universal Resource Locators (URL)/websites.

Appendix B: Small Business Resources

- National Institute of Standards and Technology (NIST)
  - Interagency Report 7621 Rev. 1 (November 2016), "Small Business Information Security: The Fundamentals"
    - https://doi.org/10.6028/NIST.IR.7621r1
  - Special Publication 800-37 Rev. 2 (December 2018), "Risk Management Framework for Information Systems and Organizations: A System Lifecycle Approach for Security and Privacy"
    - https://doi.org/10.6028/NIST.SP.800-37r2
  - "Framework for Improving Critical Infrastructure Cybersecurity" v.1.1 (April 2018) [aka "Cybersecurity Framework" (CSF)]
    - https://nvlpubs.nist.gov/nistpubs/CSWP/NIST.CSWP.04162018.pdf
- Center for Internet Security (CIS) - Critical Security Controls v.7.1, April 2019
    - https://www.cisecurity.org/controls/
- Small Business Administration (SBA) - Small Business Cybersecurity
    - https://www.sba.gov/business-guide/manage-your-business/small-business-cybersecurity
- Federal Trade Commission (FTC) - Start with Security: A Guide for Business
    - https://www.ftc.gov/tips-advice/business-center/guidance/start-security-guide-business

- ☐ Department of Homeland Security (DHS) - CISA – Home and Business
  - ▪ https://www.us-cert.gov/home-and-business
  - ○ US-Cert – Resources for Business
    - ▪ https://www.us-cert.gov/resources/business

Made in the USA
San Bernardino, CA
23 February 2020

64757770R00153